HO\
PO.......VE

Manifesting Your
Dreams

and

Discovering
Your
True Self

Richard Osborne

ISBN-13: 978-1480230750
ISBN-10: 1480230758

Disclaimer:
The information found in **How To Be Positive** is meant to
serve as strategies that are only recommendations by the
author, and reading this book does not guarantee that your
results will exactly mirror his own results. The author will not
be held liable for any unintentional errors or omissions that
may be found, or from any consequences resulting from the
use of this information.

Published by
WONDERS OF WELLNESS, Inc.
BOYNTON BEACH, FLORIDA 33426

Email: how2bepositive@gmail.com

Dedication

This book is dedicated to my grandmother, Lillian Louise Osborne. When I was a young boy she took me under her wings and shared the beauty of the written word through poetry. She opened my eyes to view the world in all its simplicity through the beauty of nature. She opened my heart to God, a power she said would always lead me where I belonged in this world.

Like the tin man, lion and scarecrow characters from the Wizard of Oz, my grandmother taught me how to have a gentle and loving heart for others, to know I had the courage to overcome life's obstacles, and the brains to believe I could be anything I wanted to be in this world.

To my children, Evan and Erica, you are my greatest gifts. This book was written to thank you both for loving me as I have loved you, in spite of the adversities we faced while you were growing up. It is your world now to go out into and make your own dreams come true.

To all the divine angels who have been there in times of need, to confirm what love, laughter, and all the precious things that make life so beautiful, are all about.

And to the many people, places and experiences that have come into my life over the years, to remind me to never lose the vision of living in this world undertaking something that enriches the lives of others.

I feel blessed and grateful to God for all of you.

Acknowledgements

My heartfelt gratitude to
Richard Bach, author of <u>Jonathan Livingston Seagull</u>, a story
that let me believe that I too could soar to heights beyond my
wildest imagination.

Oriah Mountain Dreamer, who wrote, <u>The Invitation</u> , a poem
that opens our heart in understanding the true meaning of a
soul mate, one we can spend a lifetime loving, walking hand
in hand throughout life's journey together, respecting and
honoring the commitment they have made to one another.

John Palozzi, my editor and critical advisor who guided me
through this process with a poet's eye, a writer's compassion,
and a heart and soul of gold. I will always treasure the
countless unselfish hours he dedicated to making sure I got it
right before it reached the printer.

Contents

Forward

Many of us struggle through life trying to connect with the world we live in. It begins the day we are born and for many, life is lived without ever coming to that place of belonging.

We move from one geographical location to another, seek to surround ourselves with wealth and material pleasures. We make vows to a lifetime of marriage and commit to relationships and find it so easy to run from those promises when things get a little tough. We change vocations and we even alter our physical selves as a way to fit in and bring a sense of inner happiness.

This is not what we were born to do.

What we were brought into this world to do is simple, live the life God intended for us. By this I mean to approach life every day embracing love and acceptance of thy self.
A child is born with this. Just look at the way a child goes about life and you will see how we were meant to live.

I grew up knowing where I belonged. I felt it in my heart as I watched in awe the simple beauty this world offered at every turn. The changing of the seasons, the mountains, seas, stars, sunrises and sunsets, all became reminders of how precious life is if we remain open to it and appreciative of it.

In How To Be Positive I write of my effort to get back on the right track. Whether in prose or poetry, the books I write become a guiding hand to me, a reminder that I am human and life is only as hard as I choose to make it. I pass these thoughts on to my readers in hopes they too can see what it takes to be led back to a life of genuine wholesomeness.

Many of us live never knowing our real selves. We run from the truth. We try time and time again but never really make amends with our pasts. We continue to wear masks and hide behind denial. Then one day we find a way to look at ourselves honestly and the journey to right living begins to unfold.

One does not have to be living with an addiction to sweep the truth under the rug. Confronting truth is by far the hardest thing for anyone to accept – that is why those who have fallen and begin to recover fall again.

I prayed each morning for the strength to stay on the path I was now walking. I gave thanks each night for another day of right living. Through my writing, I was reconnecting with my inner self. Through prayer I was accepting that I could not do it alone.

Then I thought it was okay to go back to my old ways...

I let myself get sidetracked from that child-like, wonderful approach to life and throw away all the good that was coming forth. I shut out the sense of belonging I had come to know through prayer.
My book was put aside. Opportunities to move forward and reclaim love, happiness and success sifted though my hands like grains of sand falling through an hourglass. Once again, I repeated the cycle. I felt undeserving. I began to lack clarity and purpose. I was feeling uneasy and insecure and stopped putting my best self forward.

As anyone who has struggled with any addiction can tell you, the road to recovery happens one day at a time.

I saw myself losing at life, jobs, finances, relationships, friends, the love of family and my own children. I knew I had to once again live my life in a different way, otherwise I would continue to falter and never be able to realize the gifts God bestowed upon me from birth.

The world throws us many curves along the way, but as I have learned over and over again, change comes from within the heart and mind.

In this book you will read the stories that have shaped my life. They are the memories I rely upon to remind me of all the people, places and experiences I have lived and learned from. Let these words guide you in your quest to reconnect with your inner self.

Embrace all that has led you to where you stand today. As you begin to accept the past and learn to let go of those things that have bound you from living a life filled with love, happiness and spiritual prosperity, you will rekindle the fire within that enables you to rebuild your life and grow your self-worth.

As you come to that place of self-acceptance, relationships with your partner, children, family and friends will be felt with renewed compassion and understanding.
As you incorporate daily prayer and gratitude into your life, feelings of guilt, anger and resentment will come to pass, opening your heart to welcome and embrace the love from others we are all deserving of.

I invite you to use this book as your guiding hand to help you attain the love, happiness and success God intended for you.

My prayer each morning is a simple one. I thank God for another day of right living, for the strength and faith that enables me to stay true to myself and to love myself once again.

Remember, one cannot love another unless they first love themselves.

Richard Osborne

CHAPTER ONE

MANIFESTING YOUR DREAMS

"Be at the helm of your own ship."

Manifesting YOUR Dream...Today, Not Tomorrow

Every dream has to have a goal and every goal has to have a purpose and every purpose has to be for the good of others in order to manifest with unlimited potential.

At 57, I am at the helm of my own ship and being guided by my Higher Power to the most beautiful destination, one I envisioned forty-two two years ago, and that is the beauty of living life its intended way.

As I revel in my own thoughts of manifestation, I ask you to do the same.

On this day, envision your dream. Find a quiet place where you can collect your thoughts and let your imagination run.

All of us have a dream.

If yours isn't coming to you right away, it's okay.

We all have a wish list.

Whatever your wish at this time in your life is, make it happen!

Making things happen in your life simply means that you are willing to accept your entitlement to something you feel will add happiness to your life, and you are willing to remove the thought barriers holding you back from achieving that entitlement.

It doesn't matter where you are right now in your life, stop procrastinating! Grab hold of that dream and set it into motion.

Excuses are the pirates of dreams!

I used to surround myself with people who could tell me every conceivable reason they can't. I made the choice to run with those who give me every reason they can!

We have two choices in life when we get to a point where we feel we have squandered opportunity; we either see ourselves as broken or see ourselves as on the mend.

We are constantly in the mending process.

Like a needle and thread stitching together a torn piece of clothing; once the rip is pulled together, the article of clothing is like new again. See yourself on the mend.

See yourself renewed and better than ever.
As I write this I think back to an eleven-year-old girl standing up on stage singing her little heart out. That young girl was given a solo in her school play, and sang "Dream, Dream, Dream."

Not long ago she called me and I could hear the sadness and hurt in her voice.

At the age of nineteen, she felt she wasn't being allowed to follow her dream in life. It seemed no matter how hard she tried to pursue what she wanted in life she was expected to take the conventional route. College is not her dream, being a singer is!

As I heard her tears fall I remembered that little girl singing her heart out up on that stage. I reminded her of a man who had to turn away from other's expectations of him to follow his own dream; the dream of being a poet, writer and published author.

I began to reach out to my daughter.

"Honey, sometimes we have to make decisions that are best for us. We do this against all wishes. In the process we may have to walk away, turn our backs on those who don't believe in us, and find an inner strength to believe in ourselves. Sometimes we need to take control of our life in spite of what others think, no matter how scared we are to do it, so that when the years pass on by, we are not standing at a place in life called regret."

Sometimes we do have to walk away from those who say they just want the best for us, but cannot find a way to let us go to pursue those dreams.

Wanting the best for someone means letting them go, setting them free, supporting their dream, and telling them no matter what, your love will always be there.

My mom did this for me when I was fifteen years old.

She took me to a place she knew would open my eyes to dream as never before. At seventeen we drove across this beautiful land of ours, arriving in our new home, where I had been awe-inspired two years earlier.

At the age of eighteen, she bid me farewell once more as I left Vancouver Island for the mainland to board a transcontinental train across Canada, to take in the majesty of the Rocky Mountains and all of that country's natural beauty.

She knew I needed to set my sights on my dream to write and she encouraged every word I penned.

She held me in her heart as she let me go each time.

When I was twenty-seven it was my time to reciprocate.

I had flown to British Columbia to spend some time with my mom. She had been diagnosed with cancer seven months earlier and I wanted to give her a dream of her own after all she had done for me in her life.

She and I took a ride by car up a mountainous path leading to the summit of Mount Baker. As we climbed higher and higher, the earth fell below and the clouds began to envelop us with a cool and soothing chill. We parked the car and began to hike across the jagged rocks until we came to a landing where we could look for miles in every direction.

I turned and held my mother's hands. As I looked into her eyes, I did not see any pain or regret. What I saw in that moment was pure peace and happiness.

I looked into those eyes and asked. "Mom, you have always allowed me to have my dreams in life, now I want you to have yours. Is there anywhere in this world you would like to go, anywhere? I will take you there."

There was no pause.

She looked right into my soul and said. "I look around, and if this is what heaven is, you have already taken me to the best place I could ever be." I realized in that moment that heaven is really here on earth.

My dear friend, AFFIRM: *"In this moment I seize heaven here on earth. I learn to embrace, and not take for granted, every single moment I am given. I take the time I have been given to climb those mountains to the dreams that await me."*

"Journey with your heart and you will reach heights of unlimited possibilities."

Never Lose Sight of Your Dream

I published my first book, INSIGHTS in April of 2011. Written in 2009, it took almost 2 years to launch. What I experienced was fear, and that is what kept me from my dream. What is keeping you from yours?

I am not certain what that fear is for you, for me it was fear of success and criticism. As one writer once told me, rejection is part of the editing process. Not editing in the sense of reworking the script, but in editing your THOUGHTS.

Quit trying to achieve the perfect ending for your dream. Don't dream with a price tag attached to it. Focus on where you see yourself belonging. If you journey with your heart, you'll reach heights of unlimited possibilities.

Success for publishing my first book was overcoming the idea that INSIGHTS had to be perfect in everyone's eyes. Once I defined why I wanted to publish my book, set aside enough for printing costs and established a date to see it in print, it manifested as it was meant to, without strings attached, without anything more than to realize a dream.

By overcoming my fear of rejection, embracing the mindset I was born with, a gift that no one could ever take away, I began to set the foundation for the dream you hold in your hands.

Whatever it is you dream, TURN IT INTO A REALITY. Remember, it is not what others think but how YOU feel.

When you feel a calling to do something know there is a divine energy or Higher Power working within; embrace it and let that energy guide and lead you to where you belong, then, let the manifestation process begin!

Once you can let go of the fear that what you want to do may not please everybody you will begin to accept yourself and see this calling as something far greater than the opinions of others. In your acceptance you will be driven to achieve.

As you put forth the effort to overcome your fears you will gain a sense of self-pride. The pride or positive energy emanating from you will begin attracting people into your life who want to love and support you in your endeavors. We are naturally drawn to POSITIVE ENERGY because it makes us feel good.

My dear friend, AFFIRM: "I eliminate the non-believers from my life, as they will drag me down and try to squash my dreams. I will not let the light of positive energy emanating from me be overshadowed by negative thinkers. I move forward and create my new way of life, and in the process turn my dreams into reality."

"*When we lose the ability to believe in ourselves, we lose our sense of purpose.*"

We Make Our Day What Our Day Becomes

I spent many years in Corporate America. I spent countless hours working and travelling, chasing deadlines and feeling the demands of my career. I needed to take my life back.

In 1997, I was asked by the New Jersey Department of Labor to design and facilitate motivational workshops throughout the state for their employees.

The jobless rate was rising and the state's unemployment personnel were burning out from the daily grind of case overload and piles of paperwork. The number of sick days taken were increasing and morale was low. Something had to be done quickly.

I gave them the remedy I had given myself. I showed them just like I am showing you, how to make your day better just by looking at it in a different light.

What we encounter in our daily lives is what we perceive our daily life to be. In other words, we manifest in our minds what our day becomes. By changing our approach we can make the day's events and circumstances work for us instead of against us.

Often we get upset because we feel like life has cheated us for our efforts. When we don't see the immediate rewards, we have a tendency to lose our self-esteem and develop a lack of confidence in our abilities.

When we lose the ability to believe in ourselves, we lose our sense of purpose. Without a purpose, we often set out in the wrong direction.

People who fail at the same thing time and time again do so because they never really take the time to reestablish their goals!

In spite of setbacks, we always need to try and remain positive in our outlook. We need to believe that everything is going to work out okay even though it doesn't seem that way at the time. I know it sounds easier said than done, but there are ways to help us achieve this. The key here is to create a daily practice that teaches us how to have a positive effect on the outcome of our day overall.

Your day should begin and end with the mindset to strive to achieve a sense of relaxation and serenity.

Begin your day by taking the weight of the world off your shoulders. Stop trying to fix the world by trying to make things happen.

As you prepare for the new day ahead, turn off the television and find a spot outside where you can sit and listen to the sounds of nature. If this is not possible, find a quiet spot in your home and put on some soft, soothing music. Try channeling into the New Age genre; my favorite is "Land of Forever" by 2002.

Now, close your eyes, take a few deep breaths, and allow yourself to embrace and give thanks for the miracle of another day given. This little moment will release you from the habitual distractions of your everyday life. These distractions can clutter your mind with a negative outlook on the day, and fog up the focus you need to look inward.

Now, focus on the calm feeling you are experiencing as you prepare yourself for this day. You definitely will see yourself in a new light. This peacefulness will begin unlocking doors that enables all the good in you to shine. Inner peace makes us that much more beautiful.

Okay, I want you to try something here. Look at yourself in the mirror now. Are you not seeing a whole new you? This new you, is the one others will see.

When you are out and about today, don't be surprised how many new people seem to come into your life. They are there because we are all naturally drawn to those that radiate with positive energy.

Don't be surprised if new doors of opportunity begin to open. A positive outlook enables you to see opportunities where none seemed to exist before. You will see things more clearly now.

My dear friend, AFFIRM: "The doors of opportunity for me existed all along, and now I have the clarity to see them. They were there for me, just waiting to be opened. Now I open them and let the new me shine!"

"A foundation built out of integrity and honesty will never collapse."

Re-defining Your Self-Worth

This is not a get rich scheme. In fact it has taken me quite a few years to define my own self-worth.

The kind of accumulation I am talking about here is wealth that enables one to live life in happiness as opposed to living in materialistic-driven grandeur.

I am the architect of my own Sky Rise, become the architect of yours.

The design was built upon a foundation of strength gained from many years of living with fewer but richer thoughts. In order to get here I had to rethink my approach to life. I had to adopt a spiritually wealthy attitude about myself. In doing so, I have been able to break down those barriers and walls that kept me from reaching my peak.

I knew in order to discontinue dismantling my aspirations I had to examine how my dreams were being built. In looking at my blueprints for life I saw certain elements that no matter how much time and labor I exhausted creating my life-scape, what I erected just tumbled down.

What I found was this.

My mindset was cemented in the belief that I was not entitled to success. I would begin to build a dream and watch it collapse. I would build again with the same results. Over and over again, I picked myself up and reconstructed and dismantled.

I actually believed that perseverance would eliminate any thought of not succeeding, when, in fact, I came to the realization that effort only works if you believe in the application. So, I went back to the drawing board.

Before I did anything I examined the materials I had to work with. I knew I had strength, courage and perseverance, picking myself up and starting over time after time showed me this. I knew I had the ability to do anything I set my mind to do, my experiences with successful undertakings proved this to me. What I lacked, because I did not prime and properly harvest it, was something far greater than all of these elements combined. I never developed fully my spiritual foundation. I believed that was to follow after the structure was completed.

Today, my life is driven by a firm belief that I alone cannot build my dream. I have come to a humble reckoning by looking to a power greater than myself for guidance. As I continue to turn my trust and faith over to my Director, I am being given more and more details for the building of a foundation held together with spiritual solidarity, which withstands the tests of will and character that caused these dreams to crumble in the past.

I also have done something I have never done before – I have raised the ceiling on the outcomes of my achievements. For the first time in my life I want to strive towards a level of spiritual wealth that will allow me to fully realize the intentions of my gifts.

I no longer want to play a small part in my life. I want to play the lead roles I have been directed to play. This is not about arrogance, it is about believing in and accepting my Director-given talents to achieve what I was put on this earth to achieve.

I say this to all my readers so that they too may tap into their natural resources, and break free from a life of mediocrity. Life does not have to be a struggle. Once you believe and accept that, set your course to identify your areas of strength and passion.

The key is to truly know where your talents lie and to love applying them everyday no matter what life throws in your path. With this passionate drive you will not allow external negativity in any form derail you from your pursuits. If you feel lost in the moment about where to begin, remember these words:

We spend our lives looking outward to find ourselves when all we have to do is look within.

I bet you never knew the answer was so close!

As you set out to discover YOU, answer these simple 2 questions:
Where does my true happiness lie?
What can I do that I love that lets me meet my obligations and responsibilities to myself, my family, friends and community?

We all have certain criteria to follow in order to be able to live a good life. When we follow the voice of our Director, our needs will be met tenfold.

My dear friend, AFFIRM: "I begin building today the foundation of a life built upon integrity and honesty. I re-evaluate the materials I have used in my past that were weak and faltered, and replace them with the strength of a belief in myself that I can rebuild my life the right way."

"Dreams are built upon intentions of creating a better world for all."

What Is It YOU Dream?

Has anyone ever called you a dreamer?

Take it as life's greatest compliment. The dreamers of this world are the ones who make the impossible happen!

They are the ones who are able to scale the walls of fear no matter how treacherous and challenging to risk everything and ultimately turn their dreams into a reality.

Dreamers, at one time in history, were seen as non-conformist who disregarded the customary way of doing things. For the most part they were considered outcasts and shunned by society.

Today, we see those same individuals as visionaries, or in more laymen's terms, "out-of-the-box" thinkers.

We have been able to redefine our attitudes simply because we now know of so many individuals who have risen above great obstacles, defied the odds and turned their dreams into a reality.

So, how do you make your dreams a reality?

First and foremost is to ask yourself what your intentions are for following your dream. Look within and picture yourself at the pinnacle of success. See yourself standing atop that mountain of your dream.

Are you able to see just what it will take to reach that plateau?

Are you willing to sacrifice all that is needed to see it through to completion?

Is your vision one that never loses sight of expressing gratitude and humbleness with each step on your way to success?

Are you willing to let go of all the vices keeping you from thinking with clarity?

Are you able to eliminate negative thinkers whose thoughts and opinions have drained you of your self-esteem and led you away from what you truly want in this life?

Can you put your faith in your Higher Power to lead and guide you once you have mapped out your course for achieving your dream? And last, but not least, set the course of your dream so that it can be carried on to help others achieve their own dreams? By giving something of value back, your success will inspire others to do the same.

Those who pursue dreams with relentless energy, defy the odds imposed on mediocre thinkers. They turn the odds in their favor though the belief that this dream is their higher calling.

My dear friend, AFFIRM: "In this moment I set my course for making my dreams come true. They are mine for the taking."

CHAPTER TWO

DISCOVERING WHO YOU ARE

"Sometimes we go somewhere in life that helps us discover who we really are."

Sights, Feelings, Words

Wind Swept Sea – The Dawning

Wind-swept sea,
Sand castles and memories.
So much I can see of myself through
these pale-blue skies,
I often wonder…
"If only I had wings to fly."
I look to the heavens and see, seagulls in flight,
Ah, what a beautiful and breathtaking sight.
I stare out at the horizon where,
somewhere, far away lies the end,
A still, quiet mystery.
My eternity begins on this day,
as my eyes meet the endless, rolling sea.
-- 1971

At the age of fifteen, I was sitting on the beach along Dallas Road in Beacon Hill Park, Victoria, British Columbia.

I'd travelled over four thousand miles to find the place I would call home two years later. A place where those very sights on that day became the feelings I write of today, forty years later, thirty-four hundred miles away.

As the seagulls swooped and soared above me, grazing the cresting waves with their wingtips, I began to feel as if I too could fly. As improbable as it sounds, when I closed my eyes I was able to break free from the constraints of a world that up until then had led me to believe I would never see my dream of being a poet manifest. (Thank you Jonathan Livingston Seagull for showing me otherwise).

In that very moment I pulled out my composition book and wrote the original version of Wind Swept Sea.

In 1973, I returned to the beach on Dallas Road and watched the flocks of gulls soaring once again. How ironic it was the very same year I began to call this place my home a man named Richard Bach wrote a book that captured it all so perfectly.

I sit upon a different shoreline nowadays, yet those very same feelings I had years ago create the same thoughts today as I had back then. You see, it doesn't matter where we go in this life, there is one certainty – you will come across a place in a time that is forever ingrained in your mind.

No matter where I have travelled, I've seen the likes of Jonathan, swooping and soaring, untouched by the pull of gravity or the fear of taking a risk to claim their dreams.

Those sights that become embedded in our heart become our feelings, which become everlasting memories. The place and time may be different when those memories reappear, but there is one constant, the images of those memories never change.

It has taken me 57 years, 49 of those waiting to realize and come to the conclusion of just why I was put on this earth.
In my life have been many trials and tribulations, heartaches and pains, felt and done unto others.

In my journey I have seen just how, by the grace of my belief in a Higher Power, I can rise above any obstacle or adversity I face.

In my life I have known that by my own actions I created my outcomes, some that carried me soaring like gulls across the great waters of existence, others that fell, so that I might see the truth of not living right by myself and others.

Seven months ago I was given an insight to undertake a new way of looking at my life. That way was in the form of this book. It has proven to be a godsend. The words I have written have shown me more about life than I could ever imagine.

My messages have allowed me to open up to my true being. As I read each word, I was reminded of just what I had to go through to get to this place and just what I need to do in order to remain on this course and fulfill my dream. .

I have since returned to that same spot where I first witnessed a beauty for life and nature I had always known existed. I knew this because I have always believed God created a special place for each of us to call home.

<u>*Memories of Victoria*</u>

I write to you my dear friend, in the quiet of this night while there is stillness in my heart and the sound of soft breathing upon my lips.

My mind filled with the wisdom of words written long ago, the image of loving memories held against my chest, the caressing of the wind upon a distant shore, and a feeling of purity and peace within.
I write to you my dear friend because I have come to a place in my life where I hold back no secrets, for fear of failing at being honest with myself and chasing away the beauty of truth with that openness.

I write to you my dear friend no longer questioning my desires to live as I have longed to live for many years, and that is as I am. For I know now that I am all those gifts I have kept locked away, with the exception of a glimpse at what could be.

Now I see what is, and I am fully alive, wanting nothing more than to set free all I was given at the time of my birth.

I write to you my dear friend so easily now, having allowed myself to feel the freedom that rings deep within my heart, to be able to express goodness and love that stirs my existence in this beautiful world.

I now see my dream as each word exits upon this page, that dream of once believing that someday I will be where I want to be, now becoming the unfolding before me as not "someday I will" but as, "I have now become that which I longed."

I write to you my friend because I can do so without question in my own mind and in yours.

You have given me your gift of acceptance as no other before you.

I know the sea was put before my eyes, its sands beneath my feet, its horizons free of my grasp, so that I may live my gift of love in words through the hearts of all they touch.
– 2/7/2011

My dear friend, AFFIRM: "In this moment I think about that place I go in my life to rediscover who I am, and take the time to revisit it every time I begin to feel lost."

"The simplicity of nature is the nourishment of the soul."

Connecting With Nature and the Soul

The Birds and The Bees

The birds and the bees
The flowers and the trees
The stars at night
The skies so bright.
The brisk spring air when blowing gently
Will pick you up and take you away
To a far off place on another day.
You will stay there from now until then
And come back never, never again.
-- 1963

I wrote and published this poem at the age of eight. The words connected me to the world at a time I felt very much alone. As much as I played the part of a kid to the outside world, I felt like an adult living in a very isolated one.

The poem speaks of serenity and simplicity, describing nature and the freedom to go anywhere we choose. The ending lets us know it is so important for us to go to that far off place from time to time to renew ourselves. It simply tells us that when we can see the beauty within, we will see beauty in all else, and with that approach to life, we will never have to go back to that old way of living again.

Throughout my life, nature and the feeling of being free as a bird inspired me to rise above life's obstacles. Embracing this freedom let me see this world and its inhabitants the way it was intended; a world filled with peace, harmony and simple beauty. Like most of us, there were times I would lose sight of my journey and true purpose for living in this world. What we really lose sight of, is the child within.

Sometimes children have no choice but to grow up. They are thrown into adult responsibilities as a result of circumstances they have no control over. Divorce, separation from familiarity, and the loss of a loved one impedes natural steps of childhood. The progression from the wonder years to an adult becomes a blur. In the process, all of these unique experiences are lived quickly, stored and saved for release later on in life.

Often the recall of these memories throw us off balance as we get older and we do not quite know how to recapture them in ways that benefit us and help us grow. We try to sweep them out of our lives and move past them as if they never transpired or, we may have others in our lives telling us our past has nothing to do with where we are right now!

I do believe from my own experiences that we are given these trials and tribulations as stepping-stones to be used in helping others. By letting our self stay connected to our childhood no matter how pained we may have felt, no matter how much resistance we met along the way, we can, as adults, recreate those experiences in a way that lets them flow like autumn leaves through calm waters.

When you become troubled by childhood memories, think of the child who will sit for hours focusing on the simplest little things, like watching clouds form incredible shapes.

Though it may seem in the eyes of the onlooker a child is withdrawn and locked into a world of their own, their world is actually one of self-reflecting and quiet thought. This was my world, those times of solace and quiet reflection helped me face the pains of my childhood.

When was the last time you just walked the beach combing for shells or ventured along a wooded path feeling the crinkle of leaves underfoot? The simplicity of nature is the nourishment of the soul. Nourish the child inside of you today.

When I feel lost, I look inside my soul and embrace the child in me once again.

My dear friend, AFFIRM: "I take the time today to reflect on those moments I loved as a child, the ones that let me explore and become mesmerized by the simplest of things. Now I go out and relive those wonderful memories."

"Make the most of each moment you are given."

Embrace This Moment

Wind Swept Sea – The Eclipse

My soul began its journey here, where
My eyes met the endless sea.
Surrounded by the soft blue sky,
The silver-winged gull that passed by
Made me believe I too could fly.
I was young then.
I was young when I believed everything lasts forever.
Wind-swept sea
Sand castles and memories
A grain of sand where once stood a sand castle.
It's all in the wind now
It's all in the wind now…
– 1973

I remember so clearly that moment and place thirty-eight years ago when I penned the words to, Wind Swept Sea. It was one poem then. It was a time when my life was awakening to a world of endless possibilities, a time when my dreams seemed like they would never elude me, a time when my wings were as strong as the wind beneath them.

As I stood watching that endless horizon, my life unfolded so clearly before me. I knew then there was nothing I couldn't do if I put my mind to it. The world was in my hands.

Then I let my life take a turn in the opposite direction, and my dreams began to fade. They faded not because they weren't real, but because I felt I had to live my dreams through the eyes of others. Unfortunately their dreams were not my own.

My dreams seemed to linger by my side for many years without coming to be. Then, one day I began to see the truth.

By looking honestly at myself, I began to see a truth about me. A painstaking reality that opened my eyes to stop living a lie I had lived for many years.

All those years I'd spent more time waiting for the next sunrise without embracing the one before me. In all those years, before I came to see what I was doing to myself, robbing myself and others of a God-given gift, I remained hidden behind a facade of denial.

We have all wished at times that tomorrow would get here quickly and put an end to what we can't deal with today. The truth is, whatever we try to escape or run from today will still be there tomorrow. This mindset denies us the beauty of living life as it was given to us to live; in the moment.

<u>Wind Swept Sea</u> was rewritten two years ago to capture the reality of what happens when we take life for granted.
<u>Wind Swept Sea, The Eclipse</u> captured the reality of life. It's words speak of our human vulnerability and the reality of our need to wake up at some point and start living the right way again, free of our past and the fears holding us back.

The castles you built may have been washed away but that doesn't mean you cannot take hold of your life in this moment and begin rebuilding your dreams.

I spent many years waiting for tomorrow to get here so I could forget mistakes I had made the day before. Today I love and live in every moment of life that I am blessed with, and when I feel the earth beginning to crumble beneath me, I say a prayer for the strength to add one more grain of sand to the life I am rebuilding. This gives me a new lease on life. Let it give you one as well.

My dear friend, AFFIRM: "I look within and ask myself today what I can do to take my dreams off hold and put them into motion. I ask myself what is holding me back, confront it, and then resolve to let it go. Instead of wishing for tomorrow to erase today, I use today to create a better tomorrow."

"Embrace opportunities as journeys of discovery about yourself."

Building Your Dreams Takes Time

Often in life obstacles and setbacks cause us to feel a sense of weakness and even hopelessness. Trust in the test, for it is in these times our greatest strengths are uncovered and become our way of prevailing over all that could befall us.

While your head is spinning over something that set you off course, remember there is a reason for this. Take the time to look inside instead of unleashing anger, resentment and blame on others. While the reason for such circumstances may not be clearly present, trust in the process of time, by allowing oneself to exercise patience and letting go.

The energy we expend trying to analyze the whys of things could be better applied to accepting this simple reasoning: "It just wasn't meant for me." In acceptance, we find truth and in truth we unlock the doors to even better opportunities.

We have been programmed from a young age to meet responsibilities and obligations and to satisfy our external world.

As we grow older, we take on more responsibilities and even greater obligations to satisfy. This is where any disruption in our daily routines of meeting those deeds causes us to feel we have failed.

But is it the failure of self, or of others?

As you approach today, stop and ask yourself this question: "If I were truly living my life, being my true self to me and others, would I not meet all that is expected for survival in such a way that any setbacks would only make me a stronger person?"

When we partake in anything with the conviction to be honest and forthright and it crumbles before our eyes, isn't it caused by external circumstances out of our control?

And when our efforts are not forthright and things go wrong, can we not find cause within our own actions for this occurrence?

When something goes awry in your life instead of asking yourself if there was anything you could have done differently to change the outcome, come to a greater plateau within by seeing it as a release from something that was not meant to be in your life at that time.

Years ago I had this outlook regarding work. I was willing to try anything just to experience what it was like. I have done many things in my life and rather than spend my time wishing I should have done things differently, I have come to accept my experiences as life classes.

As I was growing up, I saw these teachings as things I did not fit in to or things I did not want to do. Without my experiencing them, I could not have concluded this.

Now that I am older, I have done enough of the things I know I do not want to do to be able to understand what I do want to do.

For those of you who feel your life has been many wasted opportunities, try looking at it as a journey of discovery. Success in life comes from believing in this simple phrase:

You are exactly where you're supposed to be right now.

My dear friend, AFFIRM: "I accept my place and pace in this world. As I work in a way that I feel comfortable, I will accomplish even greater deeds. As I calm my mind and approach everything diligently, I will find there is less need to redo my work, and in the process I create a more rewarding life."

"Listen to the voice of your Higher Power and you will find your calling in life."

Live To Be True To Yourself

When I began to pen the words to my first book, my purpose was to give something of value to my children, most importantly, love from a father who spent many years living in a pain too deep to appreciate the gift of love they had given me just by being born.

On December 8, 2003, eight months to the day I woke up in the trauma unit of Morristown General Hospital, having been given another chance at life, I finished writing the original version of this book.

I wrote the first book as a reflective journey to capture the years I let slip, the time in my life I had gone from knowing where I belonged in this world to the times I had given up on living. The night I crashed into that wall was supposed to put an end to the years my family had suffered and free them of my self-destructive ways. Instead, I was given salvation so I could forgive myself and turn things around and see that through clarity, I was entitled to love, happiness and success in life.

I cannot tell you exactly why I pulled out the original version of <u>HOW TO BE POSITIVE</u> and began to rewrite it when I did, the universe has that answer.
Perhaps it was the need for a reawakening, a reconnecting, or simply to exercise my gift for the benefit of others. Whatever the reason, it was a divine one I did not question.

While you may question why things happen when they do, be assured it is all part of a greater plan, one that will bring answers if you can just let go and believe the outcome is part of your unique journey.

My journey was to come to the realization it was time to be honest and tell my children the story of a man they never got to know. It was my time, after thirteen years of hiding behind my pains, to open up, let go, and share the heart and soul of the man that had let his past prevent him from living and loving them as they deserved.

In the two weeks it took to write the original version I felt an incredible surge of energy running through me. I wrote day and night never feeling fatigued or at lost for words. I learned in that time that if we are willing to seek the truth, the truth will emerge in one form or another.

Truth for you may come as a need to make a change in your way of living. Only you can decide what you need to alter in order to live fully.

The moment I was able to accept the truth about myself the weight of years of unfulfilled living were lifted off my shoulders. As the last words filled the page, I began to feel emotions come over me, real heartfelt emotions no longer hidden behind fear. The tears that flowed came from a power far greater than I had ever known.

It was in that moment I revealed to myself what I had longed to see for many years. It was in that moment I gave my children the greatest gift of love I could ever give them…the real me.

Many of us live in a lie. This poem came about in my time of reflection, discovery and acceptance of the truth. Its words opened my eyes to see that rather than fight the life I was given, I needed to right the life I was living.

<u>*Hidden Behind A Facade Of Untruth*</u>

Living in a world of surreal lies
I did not know where I belonged.
I played the part of mere existence often
I played that role very well.
Yet my heart reminded me this was not living life
This was waiting for my life to begin.
Words poured easily from my emotions
Yet they were not practiced though daily living.
So easily those words were forgotten
And so readily they were discarded to be rewritten
In another time and place when
I thought I had the keys in my hand
To what I believed was the door I was to open.
So quickly I betrayed not only myself, but others
In the long run I would cast again into the void of uncertainty.
Repetition became tiresome and painful.
I could not fight for what I believed in
I was too weakened from having to face reality over and over again.
Only with the willingness to let go
And surrendered myself as ruler over my outcomes
I was able to see the light shining within.
And in the awareness I found
Something unique, something so simple
In that awakening, I discovered who I really am.
Embark upon the beginning of each new day in your life by embracing this thought:

The unfolding of our true self is the result of the journeys we take in an effort to discover who we really are.

I believe that with a clear mind and the willingness to accept the unfolding of our honesty, we can all see just why certain things happened in our lives. This is a good thing.

From my own experience, I know it may not be something we can go through without emotional pain or hurt, but it is something that will free us from nagging questions of uncertainty and the weight of denial. Once we allow ourselves to look life square in the eyes, we are able to see a clear reflection of what we could not have seen before. This becomes the truth about ourselves that we have been seeking all along.

By casting aside things clogging your thinking, the undefined circumstances in your life begin to take on meaning and application for everything that has transpired, good and not so good. Thus you can learn to appreciate every road you have travelled to get where you stand today.

Are you willing to look life square in the eyes?

In this unfolding you will be amazed at how things about your current life are happening for a reason. In this discovery you will come to accept that is was you who made the choice, you who made the decision, you who took the action to cause the outcome that resulted, or as I like to call it, the journey you embarked upon.

Remember, if the journey you are now on is or is not working, there is a reason for it. Define this journey simply by retracing your steps and you will know how YOU want to travel life's roads.

My dear friend, AFFIRM: "In this moment I reassess my journey. I look at the road I am travelling on right now and ask myself if this is really the one I wish to continue on. If life is not working for me, there is a divine reason. That reason is a simple one, I am lost! In truth with myself I will find the reason why I am unhappy. I am strong enough to face and accept the truth I reveal, and do something about it. Otherwise I will continue to walk a path not meant for me."

CHAPTER THREE

LEARNING TO FORGIVE

"Live and love life in this very second and you will live life to the fullest."

Reminiscing and Forgiving

<u>In My Alone Time</u>

On this day, in this moment
In your part of the world
I hope you are having the time of your life.

On this day, in this moment
In my part of the world
I am having the time of my life just being alone
With thoughts of you.

I wish for you to find the simple goodness in life
In front of a soothing fire.

I wish for you to hear the beauty of the world
As you listen to the waves walk upon a distant shore.

I wish for you the tenderness of a hug
From a warm and cherished friend.

I wish for you the true warmth
Of a smile from a new found one.

I wish for your day to go better
Than you ever imagined.

I wish for you a day filled with childlike discovery

From the very first moment you awaken.

I wish for you to feel refreshed and invigorated as if
You've bathed in a magical fountain of eternal bliss.

I wish you these extraordinary things simply because
You have always been that special to me.
– 2009

We never know in life when the moment to love that special somebody, to befriend someone who we have just encountered, or forgive one we have broken away from for a period of time, may pass us by never to return. If we wait until the right time, we are taking this very moment we are living in for granted.

Families quarrel, siblings fight and friends part ways, often for many years, without ever speaking to one another. I have seen this in my own family.

A mother or father who does not agree with your choices in life may turn away from you or you from them. A spouse who feels animosity towards their in-laws may create a wall between their husband or wife and their parents. Brothers and sisters may part ways over family matters. Friends may offend one another in some way causing years of friendship to unravel.

Often we feel hurt, perhaps angered and betrayed, by that separation. For some that pain lingers for a long time. That time to make amends for you could be many years. If you are waiting for the other person to reach out to you instead of you making the effort to reach out to the other person, the making of amends will never have the opportunity to transpire. We are reluctant to reach out because, well, let's face it, the hurt has cut so deeply and we fear being hurt again.

Cuts do heal over time, they may leave a scar but that mark does not have to be a reminder of anything more than our strength to overcome and heal.

I have heard many stories of regret from others who said, as much as they wanted to, it was now too late to make amends. Whatever happens to us in our lives, there is always room for forgiveness. We may not be able to sip from the same cup of happiness and share the love that first brought us together, but we will surely heal by offering up a toast of forgiveness. When we can do this, we not only take a huge weight from our hurting heart, we begin to heal the heart of the one that has hurt us.

Let us not be afraid ever to forgive and ask to be forgiven, as this becomes a new light upon the darkness in which we find ourselves living.

If you find yourself walking along a distant path reminiscing a love, friend or family member from the past, make a copy of one or both of the poems in this chapter to share with them.

The Path We Walk, In Separate Worlds Together

As I travel the path we used to walk together
I think of you and how you are walking along your new path.
I hope we hear the same sound of the ocean we used to hear
Even though the waves now crest upon different shores.
Sometimes the world is filled with a silent time
An alone time that gives us the opportunity to stop the world
Get off and see just who we really are.
You and I always reached
For that unreachable star together
But never were quite able to grasp it.
Perhaps now, we will reach it
In our own world and in our own time
And when we do

I know we will be happy for one another.
– 2003

Forgiveness is always the key no matter what becomes of those relationships.

My dear friend, AFFIRM: "Today I reach out to those I have hurt or who have hurt me, to ask and give forgiveness. I make amends and set free the guilt that has held me back from living a life filled with happiness and love."

"Weave beautiful memories into the strands of your life."

Making Amends

Woven Memories

There sits in the shadow of my long lived life
A memory woven from the time you and I were in love.
It sits there like a photograph
Unscathed by the years that have passed by
Untouched by the others we have loved
Through all the years of our lives.
Perhaps it is the season
The song or the place
That helps me to so easily
Remember your face.
Wherever you are on this day
In this time
I want you to know
Your presence in my life
Made my soul shine.
Could this day on my calendar
Have meant something to us on a day
That has long passed through time?
Was this the day long ago
When I fell in love with you and
Asked you to be mine?
So many years have come and gone since then
And though my memory is not what it used to be
I can still feel how much I loved you
And you loved me.

I will never forget the memory woven
From the time we fell in love
I will always feel you loving me
Even from the heavens above.
– 2008

People will come and go in our lives just as time will pass us by quicker than we could ever imagine. One day we may find ourselves sitting somewhere alone reflecting upon our lives and those we came to know and love along the way.

This is all a part of the human experience of growing.

In our quest to grow, we often leave behind someone or something we love very much in order to free ourselves and be open to the opportunity of a new meaning in our lives. Just as we have done this for ourselves, it is understandable, though not always easy to take, when someone we love needs to go their separate way in order to grow as well. Often we try to fight this decision, and the outcome of our reluctance to let go causes an even greater bitterness and hurt when the time finally comes to leave or be parted from.

In life and in relationships, the truth often hurts, but it is in trusting and knowing we will be better, that the hurt eventually goes away. The feelings of anger and resentment are replaced with forgiveness and understanding. A brighter light leads our way to new meanings of love and self-growth.

The light that guides us now was always there; it is the one that never faded.

If you allow that energy to be a feeling of compassion in all areas of your life, you will somehow find a way to see through what may not seem clear at the time, to a place that lets you embrace and respect the decisions you or another makes in order to grow and become a better person.

In the end, you will be able to give and receive an even greater gift of love and friendship because of the willingness to accept things as they are. In doing this we allow change to take place and because of our willingness to accept, that change will always be the best thing that could ever happen.

Life's situations and relationships do not always turn out the way we plan. Try and remember that what we may think as failure in that moment in time actually helps us to grow, opens new doors of opportunity and lets us see more clearly just what it is we want out of life. By holding on to anger and resentment, we prevent our new life from unfolding.

Embrace the faith and belief that the time away, and the growth that takes place, is all happening to bring us back to that very place we left for all the right reasons in the first place.

When all is said and done and we come full circle in this world, the transformation that has taken place lets us make amends and be thankful for what we shared. Love for someone never stops, it just takes on a new direction and meaning.

My dear friend, AFFIRM: "I believe in letting go, or in acceptance of another's decision to let me go. In this acceptance the answers I may not have in this very moment will make themselves known. I trust in that. In the long run my true rewards will prevail, giving me even more than I had before."

"Speak with a loving voice and people will listen to what you have to say."

Cleansing Through Emotions

The hardest thing I ever had to do was to tell my children I was leaving.

I watched my thirteen-year-old son get up without saying a word, walk into the next room and shut the door. I went in after him. He had his back turned to me.

I turned him around and held him.

"Son, it is okay to cry when you feel pain. The strength of a real man is not in how strong he can hold back his emotions but in how compassionately he can show them."

Emotions are the cleansing of our soul.

Everyday circumstances bring about an array of feelings. While it may not always be possible to release them in that moment, it is vital to our health to have an emotional outlet.

Love, happiness, pain, anger and fear are the five main foundations the rest of our reactions are based upon. If we do not find or create a constructive release for the negative emotions, we bring about even deeper degrees of release that will work against us. Let us look at what I mean.

Pain is usually brought about by an occurrence in our lives that causes us to feel as if life has blindsided us.

Physical pain is something we can endure. Emotional pain on the other hand, sends us reeling back as if we've just been sucker-punched. Most people do not like to intentionally inflict pain, so they become creative and use methods that bring their point straight to our hearts, sometimes without even having to look us in the eyes.

Anger can be conveyed much in the same way.

Without direct contact, we feel hopeless because we cannot express the impact of the pain and anger at the source that inflicted it upon us.

How often have you found yourself with nowhere to turn with your side of emotional release, and lashed out at some innocent bystander?

As I mentioned in the beginning of this writing, having a constructive outlet to release our emotions is the key to healthy living.

Once we are able to identify that source, whether it is walking along the ocean, having a shoulder to lean on, or just inner reflection, we are able to calm the intensity of our pain and anger, and a sense of happiness begins to pour in.

Think of happiness as sunshine and anger and pain as dark clouds. Once those dark clouds have dissipated, the sun comes shining through.

Where does fear tie in to all of this?

Think of a time you felt pained or angry with someone but were reluctant or afraid of being honest about your feelings. We do this because we have been pained and angered and do not want to inflict those feelings on someone else for fear of hurting, or in some cases, losing them.

Communication breakdown is the result of fear. Good, honest communication comes about when love guides us, not pain or anger.

Remember hearing, "We always hurt the ones we love?" How about a different way of putting this? "When we love someone, our honesty may hurt, but in the long run that love will be the greatest healer of the heart."

To live your life in health, happiness and without fear, try living with a loving attitude in all situations. When pain causes you to be hurt, look at the other person through the eyes of love and compassion. You will begin to realize they are feeling an even greater pain than what they thrust upon you.

When you are angered by words or actions someone has thrown at you, find a loving understanding within that lets you see they are suffering from difficulties they cannot handle. With this approach, your love will allow you to release your emotions in a positive way. Once released you will feel cleansed and whole again.

I have a dear friend who conveyed this wonderful way of handling someone shouting at her. Rather than get into a battle of decibels, she lowers her voice to a whisper. The other person, not being able to hear what she is saying over their own shouting, begins to lower their voice. The shouting match is never given a chance to happen, and the door to a real line of communication is opened.

My dear friend, AFFIRM: "I speak with a soft tongue, airing only love from my words. I make the divine effort to diffuse the things that have caused confrontation and stress in my life. If I meet resistance, I simply put my hand up, excuse myself, and walk quietly away."

"Make the effort today to leave behind everlasting memories."

Weaving A New Life Out Of Old Memories

We all have a past that at times we wish we could go back and do over, that is, if we have lived life! I certainly have mine!

As I was growing I never really gave any thought about how my selfishness could hurt others. Sometimes we have to learn the hard way but it is never too late to learn.

As we live our life it is evident we leave a trail in our wake. This is the inevitable part of growing in our society. Each day brings about new experiences and encounters with people, places and things.

As invisible as we may try to be, we always leave something behind. In our journey we leave behind some everlasting memories, some we cherish and some we try for years to forget.

After my divorce, I lived with years of guilt. I became distant and withdrawn from my children, not because I stopped loving them, but because I felt I had failed them. What I failed to see was the pains they were experiencing as I pulled away.

Life isn't perfect nor are we.

The Road Up Ahead

As I walk the roads set before me
I will never turn back and let the pains of yesterday
Keep me from my journey.
I will look instead to that, which awaits me with great enthusiasm.
I will take a moment each day to look back in my mind
To give thanks to all those whose lives have touched mine
Making the road up ahead that much easier to travel.
– 1981

If we hang on to yesterday, we never allow ourselves the opportunity to welcome the new gifts that await us. Dwelling in the past, feeling sorrow or resentment over that which we wish we had done differently, only keeps us cemented in all that was, instead of freeing us up to embrace all that is and can be.

It took me a long time to realize no matter how much I prayed to turn back the hands of time and redo my life, asking to go back and fix what had already passed was holding me back from living life as it was meant for me.

The beauty of this growth and evolution is the experiences we encounter and how we choose to live them. If we live life in fear of making mistakes, we live a very sheltered existence and never afford ourselves the chance to get it right.

I was trying to be perfect; to emulate others I thought had it all down pat. I was trying to be something or someone that was not me. I made my share of mistakes.

I may have run and hidden, but found out, solitude, no matter how many miles away you seek it, never takes the fear of failure at something or the reality of hurting someone you love and care about, away.

No matter where you wind up, that weight stays with you. It stays there as long as you refuse to see it, understand it, take responsibility for it, and start living with integrity and begin applying right action and genuine concern for the wellbeing of others.

As I have set aside my past to embrace this moment, this day and this new approach to life, I realize it is so much easier to forgive others when we have forgiven ourselves.

We are human and we will stumble along the way leaving imprints that leave scars. We often spend years living with those scars, trying desperately to reinvent ourselves in hopes they will disappear. The scars we have ingrained will never vanish completely.

Through our honesty and good faith efforts to make amends with ourselves and those we have hurt, the scars will eventually become fine lines of beauty, healed by our goodness and right action.

Making these amends tests our wills and perseverance. As we set forth on our journey to right our wrongs, we are often met with resistance from those unwilling to forgive.

We may not be able to win back every heart we have hurt, but even from a distance, we will be able to hold our heads high knowing we made the effort to make amends.

As we ask of others to forgive us for the pain we have caused, we must, without hesitation, be willing to forgive those who have pained us.

My dear friend, AFFIRM: "Today I make amends with those I have hurt. I accept they may not be willing to listen, but I know in my heart I am forgiven, and can let go of this pain in my life."

CHAPTER FOUR

AWAKENING THE POSSIBILITIES

"There is something that guides you spiritually."

Tapping Into Your Higher Power

I am sure many of you are into some form of religion. Even if your foundation or belief doesn't encompass a set sect, I am certain there is something that guides you spiritually. And if you choose not to associate any kind of Higher Power with your existence at this time in your life, perhaps this writing will at least get you thinking.

I am certain there will, if there hasn't already been, a moment in your life when you will feel the need to call upon something to help you out. This calling is a crying out, a humble realization that in times of desperation, we want to connect with a source that will provide guidance, strength and encouragement.

When I worked in the field of mental health, I was entrusted to lend an ear and be a friend with a heart that would show compassion. This is a gift. Throughout my life, this gift has not only helped me help others, it has saved my soul many, many times.

Sometimes we find ourselves in a state of despair, or in medical terms, a state of depression. We may feel life has become overwhelming and there is nowhere to turn. Oftentimes in this frame of mind we are afraid to ask for help. What transpires eventually during this period of darkness is a desire to isolate or shut the world out.

Although it may not seem easy to understand, isolation or withdrawal is done as a way of protecting oneself from further pain. The person going through a state of depressed feelings becomes afraid to reach out to others for fear more pain might ensue.

We are in a vulnerable state.

We develop a fear that others may not understand our needs so we keep to ourselves.

I am aware that someone reading this who has a degree in mental health may jump out of their chair and dispute this statement.

What I am presenting here is not related to a chemical imbalance; I am addressing the absence of a trusted spiritual and human support system to be there in times of emotional need.

We all need somebody to lean on at some point in our lives.

Now, let's get back to the acceptance of a Higher Power or spiritual guidance as a means of direct communication in times of trouble.

Prayer in any form is simply a request to be heard.

What happens next is up to you.

There are two choices here.

You fight it or you let go.
To fight is to resist, push away or combat.

Let me ask you. "Does it make sense to ask for help and then prevent it from entering your life?"

It is like running to the emergency room to get stitches to close a wound and when the doctor begins the procedure, you up and run out. Doesn't do much for your bleeding wound does it?

Letting go means simply; you trust your call for help has been heard and is being taken care of.

In 1980, my grandmother presented me with a book written by Albert E. Cliffe entitled, Let Go and Let God. For many of us this represents a way of living…letting go and letting God.

The basis for many of my writings have centered on accepting the things we have no control over in life, and just releasing them to a Higher Power to take care of.

Cliffe was a biochemist who turned from his work to become a layman of the church. He became a leader in the movement of spiritual healing within the organized church.

As I read through the pages of his book, I felt an inner revelation take over.

I began to discover a truth so many of us fight in our quest to find out who we really are.

We often stand at the doorstep of realization and fail to absorb the message Cliffe uses in his title, Let Go and Let God.
As simple as the message these few words imply, we often overlook them in our search to find real meaning in our lives.
For some reason, we choose to cloud our minds with complex, analytical analogies, instead of simple remedies. We fill our bodies with antidotes that divert us from a natural healing. We feel we must delve with a microscopic eye into the organisms of beauty, rather than seeing it as intended in its true form.

Modern technology is truly remarkable, but let me remind you of life's simplicity.

While we have the scientific capability to look at the molecular structure of a rose, it is a much greater pleasure for the soul to capture its exquisiteness as a stem reaching upwards from the earth and unfolding its glory in the late afternoon sun.

God as a divine spirit, or wherever you have come to believe your spirituality comes from, asks us to let go and put our faith and trust in relinquishing our obstacles to such beliefs. We do this to take the weight off our shoulders, and accept resolution of our problems will come as it should, in our best interest.

By letting go we begin to unfold our inner beauty. The love that was once sought for self-pleasure is replaced with a desire to show our love for others. As we put others before us, with a divine conviction to help them bring out their best, we are showing the radiance of our Higher Power.

As we feel this radiance, we discover an inner happiness, one that is void of selfishness and material wants. The lives we touch are drawn to this spiritual happiness, and in turn, we are the recipients of the love that was instilled within us at birth.

When we are able to let go and let God, we accept that we really have no control over our destiny. We become willing to let our journey in this world be guided not by receiving all we can, but by giving all we can.

By entering into a peace within, we are letting go of our physical desires and embracing a higher level of consciousness. This leads us to discover the beauty of life; one we can begin and live at any age.

If you are willing to release yourself to a higher source of power, not found in any antidote, but life itself, you will open your heart and mind to welcome your greatest potential.

When we struggle with life and choose to run or hide from it, we accomplish nothing more than prolonging what we eventually must face.

Look within yourself and feel the power within. The inner goodness found will bring a glow of hope and faith to overcome anything presently holding you back.

As I sit writing this I can feel my grandmother smiling down upon me.

In her ninety-one years of life on this earth she was a true blessing to all who came in contact with her. She lived life to its fullest and enjoyed every single minute she was given. Because she was able to find beauty in all, all found beauty in her.

I ask you to seek the same in this world as she did.

Prayer does not have to be hours and hours of total redemption. It does not have to take place in any church or holy house. You do not have to hold on to or bow to symbols. I am not saying these rituals, if you practice them, are not right for you. What I am saying is: prayer can take place anywhere, anytime and under any circumstance.

Just close your eyes for a moment and ask simply that the weight of whatever it is you are carrying be lifted off of you. Then let go of it. Believe that help is already there.

I've learned over the years that things always happen when they are supposed to, not when we want them to.

When we try to force or take control of the outcome, much like a small child whining to get their way, we create a resistance to the natural order of things taking place to resolve our issues. Faith, prayer and trust are our greatest allies.

Trust in yourself even if you have a tough time believing things are going to be okay. Pray for the help you need to reclaim your life and have faith you will rise above whatever it is that is standing in your way right now.

I have a friend who has been going through some tough times lately. His world has literally fallen apart. He has fallen from the top of a very prestigious mountain of material comfort and finds himself now sitting, figuratively, in a dark, damp cave, void of all the surroundings and lifestyle he had grown accustomed to.

He came to me the other day and asked why he was feeling this way. I responded. "You lack faith and gratitude!

"How is that?" He asked.
I summed it up this way.
"My friend, envision walking on a desert for days thirsting when all of a sudden you come upon a faucet dripping tiny beads of water. In your current state of mind, because you are still living in your past, trying to hold on to all that no longer exists in your life, you rush to turn on the faucet and savor the full gush of water, rather than place your mouth under the tiny droplets and be gratified to satiate your thirst."

We all beat ourselves up from time to time. This is a natural part of looking within and finding resolve for something that didn't work out as planned.

This is how we grow.

Before I sat down to create this book I was stuck in the rut of pondering my next move. I had been laid off from my job. As the days passed I began to lose faith and fall into a pit of worthlessness. I tried to look at things optimistically and began to welcome the possibility of something new and better coming into my life. Although I was somewhat excited, my emotions drifted back and forth, often lapsing into sleepless nights and depression. It was in those wee hours of the morning I began to write down my thoughts. As each page unfolded I sensed something good happening. I had faith all was going to be okay.

And, just what is faith?

Whatever it is inside of you that gets you to rethink the process of something that did not go well is FAITH.

Whatever it is inside of you that allows you to believe that things can be turned around in your favor is FAITH.

And whatever it is that guides you, sets you at ease, and lets you know things are going to be okay, is FAITH.
FAITH is ever constant, always on the job twenty-four hours a day, seven days a week, for all of your life. You may not feel it, but it is working behind the scenes and is ready to respond when called, any time of the day or night.

By channeling my thoughts on something constructive, creative patience replaced panic, energy replace lethargy, and purpose replace worthlessness. As each word was written I could see the manifestation of something good unfolding.

When things happen in life unexpectedly, God sets in motion a new direction for us. He has other plans!

The plans He had for me were to fulfill my dream of writing this book. Once I was able to accept my loss and let go of any negative emotions I was holding, my new direction came into being.

Trust in the things in life that test our will, for it is in these times our greatest strengths are uncovered and become our way of prevailing over all that could befall us.

While your head is spinning over something that set you off course, remember there is a reason for this. Take the time to look inside instead of unleashing anger, resentment and blame on others. While the reason for such circumstances may not be clearly present, trust in the process of time by exercising patience and letting go.

The people that know me, know I have done many things in my life, and rather than spend my time wishing I should have done things differently, I have come to accept my experiences as life classes.

As I was growing up, I saw these teachings as things I did not fit into, or things I did not want to do. Without my experiencing them, I could not have concluded this. Yet, when I lost my job recently I never thought to listen to my own words.

It took some time and deep soul searching, but now I can see that all I have done in my life had a divine purpose. I had to experience what I did to know what I did not want to do, to understand what it is I do want to do.

If you find yourself feeling like life has been many wasted opportunities, try looking at it as journey of discovery. Success in life comes from believing in this simple phrase: *"You are exactly where you're supposed to be right now."*

Some of us are designed to take longer than others to discover their dreams. Enjoying the time it takes to get there and taking in everything along the way for each experience you encounter is a piece of that dream.

When you feel as if life has thrown you off course, do not despair. Use the time to think about all the possibilities and opportunities you can create for yourself. You can make lemonade out of lemons, so why not start squeezing new life into all those dreams that have been lying on the shelf for years?

My dear readers I am open to hear what you have to say about the new dreams you discovered when it seemed all was lost.
Write me at: **how2bepositive@gmail.com**

As you will see in any circumstance that has you reeling and feeling helpless, all it takes is one call, one prayer, one moment where you stop and let go and let God. In a fraction of the time it takes to worry, fret and stress about something that in all actuality has already passed, FAITH is at your inner doorstep bringing resolve and peace back into your life.

My dear friend, AFFIRM: "I pray for the release of all that has hindered me. I let myself fall into the arms of a faith that guides and lifts me above and beyond all that has kept me from feeling peace and serenity within."

"Be of service in whatever ways God has planned for you today."

Giving Without Expectation

Acceptance and trust

When you truly love, you do not judge or question.
When you truly love, you do not impose your will or hide the truth.
When you truly love, you feel it from within
*   even when you are alone.*
When you truly love, you give all with gratitude
*   and all with humbleness.*
When you truly love, the sun is a warm hug
*   and the moon is a divine reflection of love's light.*
When you truly love, life is good no matter what happens.
When you truly love, you are truly loved back.
– 1/13/2012

There are people in this world who are in a position to help others, yet are reluctant to do so for fear they will not receive anything back. When you love truly, you give without expectations.

If you can help someone today, do it without question. By doing for others, life does reward us in so many ways. The old saying that things come back tenfold is a philosophy to live by. Adopt the "pay it forward" concept today and see just how your life is changed for the better.

I wake up every day looking for ways to give of myself to others. What I find is that when I make myself available to help others, the things I ask my Higher Power for in times of need come automatically. I may not see the results of my efforts right away, but I know they are just over the horizon waiting for the right time and place to unfold. I never have to ask, my needs are met as I go about my daily business of helping others.

In this very moment ask yourself how you would like to remember what you will leave behind as this moment passes from your life. Once you have defined your outcome, your actions will set the course for the results you have envisioned.

Life is really a simple act of individual actions guided by many things. If we are willing to let a power greater than us lead and guide those actions, we are certain to put forth the right energy in all our doings which will always result in the right outcome.

The confusing part for many of us is when the outcome doesn't always match our perception of what it should have been. We feel we have put forth our absolute best effort and expect the outcome to be exactly as we desire. Desire is nothing more than want, and we can't always get what we want or expect, in return for our efforts.

The key here is to know how to act in this very moment on our intended outcome. By acting out of love and unselfishness we convey this in our actions, and in doing so, create a sense of harmony and willingness amongst those receiving our intentions.

Although our intended outcome may not be realized right away, our efforts are not in vain. If our intentions are good, the outcome of our efforts will produce something good at some point, somewhere.

Once we give of ourselves the wheels are in motion for things to come back to us. It is such a simple way to live. Your gifts to others do not have to be of monetary value. Offering your time and service means lending a hand to one in need.

Find a way each day you can benefit someone as you go about your daily routine. Sometimes all it takes is a smile and a kind word to make someone feel like a million dollars.

Last week I was in my car approaching a light. The light was green and a car was sitting to my left with emergency flashers on.

As I got to the intersection, the light turned red.

While I was waiting for it to turn green again I kept looking in my side view mirror. There was a man behind me trying to get his car started. The car he was driving was a very expensive one. I thought for a moment, I am sure he can call someone to help him.

The man then got out of his car and just stood next to it. I noticed he was quite elderly and looked somewhat bewildered.

As the light turned green I began to make a left and suddenly found myself in his lane backing towards him. I put my emergency flashers on and walked over to him.

"Are you okay?" I asked.

"I can't seem to get this thing into gear." he said.

Mind you I am not a mechanic, and would never try to be anything close on a $150,000 car, but I found myself asking him to turn his car off.

I asked him to start it again.

He tried to engage the shifter to no avail.

I leaned in to see if there was some sort of a locking control or anything that may help get this car in gear. As I was looking at the instrument panel I just happened to look down at the floorboard.

"Take your foot off the gas and put it on the brake and then try to shift."

Lo and behold, it worked!

As he passed me he honked his horn, smiled and waved. I realized in that very moment, my call to service had been answered.

I have come to realize that whatever our call may be, we are well equipped to handle it.

Gratitude and love came to me that day in a honk, a smile and a wave from a stranger I took the time to help.

In transit, I see many new faces that seem as if they have been in my life since I was a child. Perhaps it is that child in me resurfacing, and the innocence of that child has me looking at love in a new way.
The great need I felt for many years, the energy I spent and the emphasis I put on the way I used to look at love, has been replaced by something far more enriching and satisfying. I see love today as a service my soul provides to others.

As I undertake a new day, a gift I am given to fulfill in the best way I can, my first thought is to give gratitude for this gift. My second thought is one of thankfulness for believing in something that has redefined love for me.

In my conversation with what I believe is my true teacher I ask only one thing, *Place an opportunity in front of me that lets me be of service.*

I do not ask for specifics, I just say I am ready and willing to take on whatever is in store.

Try this new approach to life today. Ask for nothing more than to be of service. Don't ask for anything specific, because you will be looking for that and not realize when your call to service comes.

I would love to hear how you awakened new possibilities as a result of helping others. Tell me about your "getting it back tenfold" story and I will include it in my next book.

Write me at: **how2bepositive@gmail.com**

My dear friend, AFFIRM: "I answer the call of being of service in any way possible to another. The time I take today to help someone else will be a giant step in showing others that I can give without expecting anything in return except a thank you."

CHAPTER FIVE

FOLLOWING THE WRONG GOD HOME

"Plant the seed of good in all you do today."

You Are The Planter And Caretaker Of Your Life

We are responsible in many ways for the journeys we take in this life. The outcomes and what we experience are the result of the choices we make along the way.

We are the playwrights of our lives. We have the ability to create whatever outcome we choose. By believing in what we create, we manifest its reality. This is the absolute truth.

We can learn what does and doesn't work for us if we pay attention over the years to our trials and tribulations, and to our choices. The choices I made were my teachings. Some lessons I learned quickly, others took some time. Why was that? As I searched for answers, I found myself coming to the same conclusions.

Personal growth is a process that can only be successful when we take that knowledge we seek to grow, and willingly apply it to daily living.

We can conclude as well that what we encounter in our daily life will be the result of what we perceive our daily life to be like. In other words, we can choose to make our day what our day ultimately becomes.

By changing our approach, to see everything in a positive light, we are now able to have the day's events and circumstances work in our favor.

What we begin to see are doors of opportunity opening up each day. It is not that they didn't exist; they were there all along waiting to be opened. We just had to be willing to see and open them. Once in, the rest is up to you.

Physical transition has always been a part of my life. What I was seeking was to first understand the spiritual process of transition, and then to trust it.

To help you with this, allow yourself to seek a better understanding of your Higher Power, whatever that is for you in relation to personal change and transformation.

The transition I seek is to know my divine gifts and believe in myself with such a conviction, that I arise each day and joyfully lay the groundwork, while stepping back and letting my divine guider take care of the rest.

I know with this belief I will no longer struggle with the question, "What is my purpose in this life?"

Through these actions, I accept my purpose as the planter and caretaker of the seed that grows the fruit tree. By letting go, I give my trust in God to fill that tree with the fruit it is meant to bear.

I believe we are a reflection of divine love in many ways.

Each day, if we do our best to reflect that love though a commitment to help others, we will naturally be extending the goodness that comes from love of thy self. This is known as working from the inside out.

In our effort to transition, or right our lives, from the way we have lived it unsuccessfully, we begin to let go of old thought patterns and habits.

As we step outside of our old selves and begin our journey of renewal, we create a place of being that is unknown. This can quickly fill us with fear and a desire to retreat from our plan of action. Think of it like this.

You come to the edge of a river, the water is racing by with tremendous force, and there is no bridge to cross it. The absence of a means to reach the other side creates a challenge for you.

Most of us see this as a disruption. We begin to feel fear and the desire to retreat because this is not what we expected. We expected not to have to figure a way to bridge this gap, but to have one there ready to cross.

This is the reason most people never attain real happiness and success in life.

Happiness and success comes from our ability to rise to these types of challenges. When we allow ourselves the time to think about a solution, we give ourselves the opportunity to welcome an answer.

When we let fear take over and see life's challenges as obstacles, we close off all possibilities for a solution to manifest.

It is in that absence of a means, that our lives can either be hurled into a void of uncertainty that scares us, or can take us to a place of new growth and strength.

Welcome this challenge, and in any moment of uncertainty ask yourself this question. "Why am I here?"

If you can be truly honest with yourself, you know exactly what brought you to this place in your life.

Denial of truth is an easy way to numb the reality of what we really feel.

Acceptance and honesty to our self enables us to know our actions. So why do we have a hard time being honest with ourselves?

Failure at not living up to other's expectations!

When we are conditioned to know that we will be loved, accepted and respected, no matter what the outcome, as long as we tried our best, we are allowed to feel comfortable being honest and fair in assessing our efforts. We grow up knowing we can face new challenges and rise above obstacles because we never stop believing in ourselves.

And, when we come to that raging river without a bridge, WE WILL FIND A WAY TO CROSS...

My dear friend, AFFIRM: "I am the "Leader of Encouragement" in other people's lives. I lift them up with words of kindness and motivation and I am lifted up as well."

"Look for the glisten of heaven's light in the clouds today."

When Life Becomes You

When Life Becomes You

When all is freed about you in life
When thought becomes unadulterated
Pure and void of outside influence
When your heart and soul is set afire
By emotional depth from a Higher Power
And your actions speak of truth and desire
To know only that way of living.
When you can sit upon the shore and listen
To the heartbeat of each cresting wave
When you can gaze above and see
The glistening of silver wings amongst the clouds
When within you begin to emerge without force
A gentle, loving being whose purpose
Is to be of unselfish service.
When you can vision each color of the universe brilliantly
Speak each word from your mouth with passion and not anger
When you can know yourself as you have never known yourself
And you can offer your newfound energy without fear of tiring
When you can live your dreams though the eyes of a loving soul
And share in the prosperity of its realization
Without reward in return.
When you can rise above any obstacle
No matter the pain and effort in doing so
When you truly feel you have come to your place
And yet are willing to discover and learn even more.

When you understand sacrifice
And give so knowing you will be strengthened.
When you embark on your journey in this world
And set out to enrich its existence through your own enrichment.
When you extend nothing but kindness to those along your way
And leave in your wake a smile.
When you can close your eyes at the end of each day
And feel peace and gratitude within.
You will have come to know it never really mattered
What others thought you should have done with your life.
For in that quiet moment of self reflection
You will know you have done your best.
—3/5/2012

"So, what do you think I should do?"

The more we seek opinions and answers from others to the things affecting our lives, the more reliant we become on living our lives through these sources and the easier it becomes to disregard our intuition.

As we begin to look inwards and not externalize, it is easy to understand and accept the outcome of our decision.

When we are enabling others to lead us, we find ourselves putting the outcome of our action back on them and this results in blame instead of not taking responsibility for that outcome.

Like many, I became reliant on and enabled by the opinions, suggestions, and recommendations from others. This weakened my self-esteem, and believe it or not, caused me to repeat the same mistakes over and over again.
You see, when we live through the lives of others there comes a point of rebellion that says very loudly, "I AM GOING TO DO IT MY WAY!"

This is okay. This is exactly where we need to be in order to gain back our power.

The one or ones we have broken from will probably try to lead us back into their temptation, or they may actually be relieved you have decided to take charge of your own life and outcomes.

For those who tempt you to return to THEIR way of thinking by trying to reinforce the thought that YOU cannot do it on your own, just look at them with love and say, "I know I am not going to get it right the first time or maybe the second or even the third, but that is okay, just love me for having made this decision and believe it will all work out for the best."

In my present state which trusts the outcome even in times that appear uncertain, I allow myself to not try so hard to understand, but to accept a feeling of loving myself completely and letting go of knowing only good can come from living in the truth, and knowing who I am is who I am supposed to be.

I know that this comes from having come to that place in my life of letting go and letting God take care of life's circumstances I cannot control.

I now know I manifest what I choose to believe. If I see my life as a journey filled with love, happiness, exhilaration, newfound dreams, adventure and fun, I become the one to create fulfilling beginnings to everything in my life.

My dear friend, AFFIRM: "I unlock my doors of opportunity to my highest self. I know that my willingness to accept all that I am, will let me discover my highest levels of spiritual consciousness, which will freely pour forth even greater gifts from within."

"Chart the course of a lifelong dream today."

Guiding Your Journey Through Your Higher Power

Life brings with it many challenges and tests.

This is true at any age.

This is evident no matter what our standing in society may be: rich, middle of the road, or struggling just to stay afloat.

These obstacles come upon us when we are the least prepared, that is why they are deemed in a more formal definition, as tests of our will.

What is our will?

What is our wish for our ability to prevail over the challenges presented?

Initially, we all seek a means to a way out.

This is not what our Higher Power has intended us to seek.

Mountains are put in our way to be climbed, not evaded or reduced by will to smooth highways we can just cruise along without tolls to pay.

A toll is defined as something that places a strain on us, yet we travel from one destination to another paying them without reluctance in order to get to our chartered destinations. Having an E-Pass still requires one to pay for their journey.

The only way around this is to stay put and that is not going to get us anywhere in life!

Come with me as we journey willingly, take in the beautiful sights life has to offer, and see just what it takes to go through the tolls of living using your E-Pass or Enlightened Pass to success.

Imagine yourself charting a lifelong dream of sailing around the world.

As you set your course for sail, you begin to envision the many exotic destinations you will see along the way. You look over scores of pictures showing tropical paradises, rustic ports of call and historical landing points you will visit along your journey. In this moment of visual bliss your heart embraces the wonderment of God's earthen, natural beauty.

In your mind, you hear the sounds of calm waters and blue skies, nights filled with glittering heavens and golden moonlight. You see yourself standing at the bow as the sun beckons the dawning of a new day with all its brilliant colors.

You play in your mind the melody of gentle breezes blowing your hair, as the day comes to a close, guided by heaven's artistry splashing the night sky canvas with a kaleidoscope of crystal-colored brilliance.

Through the night you embrace the gentle rocking of water lulling you to deep, sound sleep. You dream of your next destination in calm and peace.

Every journey we take in life should be as this, but the courses of our existence often throws a different scenario in our way. The smooth sailing becomes turbulent. Our visions and expectations are thrown overboard by the laws of nature. Here is where our belief in a Higher Power prevails, tossing to us a preserver kept afloat by our belief in our ability to rise above the mountainous waves that have cast us into raging waters.

I once took a commercial fishing trip with my friend while I was living in Victoria, British Columbia.

From the offset, although I had been on the seas, never had I experienced an eleven-day journey of deep sea trolling in the great Pacific waters.

As I prepared, the key to what I soon faced from nature and God, I envisioned exactly the scenarios I opened my story today with. The most important aspect of that vision was summed up in one word, glorious.

In my thinking of a vast ocean, an endless horizon, the splendor of being surrounded by God-built beauty, the only thought that kept running through my mind and heart was how glorious this journey would be. I never once foresaw, nor did I even think to include in the preparation process, feelings of fear.

In that glorious moment I saw nothing but an opportunity to seize a once-in-a-lifetime opportunity, a gift to encounter something so few ever get to experience in their lives. It was that mindset and that belief that let me overcome fear and climb the mountains we faced, undaunted by any preconception of not being able to do so.

It was that spiritual guidance I heard from a voice deep within, as those mountainous waves washed over our vessel, tossing and turning us against our will, that let me see the truth of my existence. That truth let me ride each turbulent crest with the experience of a life-seasoned seafarer. The beauty engrained before I set out on my journey unveiled itself even as wind and rains pelted down upon me.

I stood at the bow on one of those stormy nights, reeling in our net, thinking not of the freezing waters across my face but of the radiant moonlight, star-filled heavens, and the catch we were about to receive.

As the net began to unfold and the fish emptied onto the slick surface, I embraced my will to stand firm and take on the task of preparing our catch for storage in the hold.

As one raised and conditioned to never hurt a living creature, I came to accept what I had to do not as going against the grain of my beliefs, but as a means of survival, being a commercial fisherman. What transpired next clearly defined a phrase I have come to make part of my daily practice, "It is only in giving that we receive."

As we had received what we needed on that trip for my friend's family to live, we had given back that which we could not use.

In the giving back, I experienced the feeling of oneness with the beauty of a bird that has come to symbolize for me the basis for transforming my dreams. (Richard Bach, if you are reading this, thank you for introducing me to Jonathan Livingston Seagull, the symbol of dreams and unlimited flight I have carried throughout these years as my inspiration for believing in my own dreams as a writer.)

The gulls began to swoop down, taking the food from my hand. Sliver wing after silver wing, illuminated by the moon's light, gently plucked the gift of the sea from my outstretched fingers. I did not feel the rain or cold, instead I felt the warm energy of these glorious creatures running through me as their beaks gently touched my hand.

As morning dawned, the waters calmed, the skies cleared and I was blessed with one of the most magnificent sunrises I had ever seen.

Untouched, it crept up on the horizon all ablaze filling me with the inspiration I use today when I blend the memories of those colors upon a canvas.

As we headed back to shore, I gave thanks for the gift of that journey. I knew the tolls I paid, the mountains I climbed, were all designed to ingrain within me thoughts that would let me relive those moments long after I had set my feet back on land.

As you prepare your own journeys in this life, see the beauty, not the calamity, embrace the colors, not the uncertainties, believe in the outcome, not fear the unknown, and you will claim the beauty and wonderment of your destiny overcoming any mountain you have to climb and any toll you have to pay to get there.

My dear friend, AFFIRM: "I see the beauty in all I undertake today. I do so without fear and welcome the challenges I face with confidence to overcome. When I feel weak, I ask for strength from God."

"In silence, you will hear the voice of comfort."

Let Your Soul Hear The Voice Within - Part 1

It is said that any idea that is to be will manifest itself in the silence of the soul. For in this silence, we will hear the answers to all we question when the world around us swallows us up in the whirlwind of haste and anxiety.

I have needed to hear God's voice but have not allowed myself the time to listen.

Always let your heart dream. Allow your mind to run free with all the limitless possibilities of that dream unfolding into reality.

We let ourselves become restricted by the daily mundane quests for survival. Even in its simplest form, survival can be a struggle. This struggle can consume us and cause us to shortchange ourselves and constrict our greatest possibilities from becoming a reality.

Dreams should be dreamt big. When you lift the ceiling of your expectations, you create a whole new horizon in which you can achieve so much more.

Before that peace can become part of your environs and physical structure of your dream, it must become a way of the mind and soul, and this is where the seeking of spiritual guidance comes in.

There is a power greater than us that will guide us to great success in our darkest moments if we just allow that energy to come into our life. When we are fighting physically to lift the weight of the world off our shoulders our minds are already working on solutions to relieve us from these burdens.

I always undertook physical tasks in my life by mustering all the muscle I could to get them done. There was never any thought involved, just physical exertion, this was how I was taught to approach work from a young age by my father.

My mother, on the other hand, told me I needed to develop my mind with my body, in order to balance out my life, live long, healthy and free of physical pain. She also instilled a balance of both through a belief in a Higher Power, one that would show me an approach I could not see through sweat and physical exertion.

When I read about the success of others and the experiences that helped them overcome obstacles, I realized they all had something in common. Successful people are able to humble themselves through the mindset that they are not greater than life itself, that there is something more powerful guiding them. It was through such humble realization that the virtues of all their successes were understood.

As the successful men and women I read about were able to see this, I too began to see it. And, you can also come to see that there is a solution for all that you are having trouble dealing with.

When you stop digging, put down your shovel and come to rest under a tree, you become a willing participant in the process of renewal. As we struggle to complete the task, we exhaust ourselves of all energy needed to complete it. We then close our natural thought process and block the insight needed to unfold solutions.

Once you start to achieve this peace, it is very easy to neglect. In order to maintain its presence, you need to be honest enough to accept calling upon a power greater than yourself to help you reclaim it.

This place of peace and unfolding can only come in the quiet and solitude of self. As you start to achieve this peace within do not neglect to maintain it. The importance of balance is essential to your continued wellbeing. Seek nature and creative expression in your daily life.

Wake up early and walk into the outside world. Watch the colors of the morning unfold and breathe the dawning of a new day. Look around, embrace all where you are in the moment in microscopic simplicity. Smile to the rising sun and be thankful of all that is.

Peace within is a natural prescription for long life. Self medicate with the wonders and beauty of nature. Even amongst the tallest skyscrapers, the bustling of people and traffic, the sun still sets and rises. In the maze of concrete jungles the rains and the snows still fall. In the blistering heat of day there is solace in the memories of a satiated thirst.

During torrential downpours that raise our rivers and lakes to the point of sweeping over our lands and washing away our existence, there is comfort in knowing we can rebuild new dreams from the ones that never unfolded.
In disruption believe in the energy of good change.
In doubt, believe in the coming of resolve.

In pain know the healing is evident.

And in all areas of your life, believe all is in divine order.

No matter how difficult it may seem at the time you are only one stepping-stone away from a path of prosperity. This path is not defined by its physical geography but by our spiritual visions.

In this spirit is held the beauty of a world created before us. We were created after it, and we were created to be messengers of the expression of that beauty.

My dear friend, AFFIRM: "I let go of what is conflicting me. I look around and see the simple pleasures and beauty of this world I live in. I resolve to appreciate nature."

"Be the shepherd of your destiny."

Let Your Soul Hear The Voice Within - Part 2

I believe that there are two types of people in this world: those who struggle to define who they are and those whom others have a hard time accepting.

When we are able to define our existence by being true to ourselves, we often meet naysayers who just cannot accept our uniqueness.

So be it!

Instead of questioning your unique existence, let it define itself to those who can understand its meaning to you, not to them. Quit battling to convince the naysayers otherwise.

Seek out those who are like you, those who see something outside that box others spend their lives hitting their heads against the walls of. Let them keep the hamster mentality that keeps them going round and round, never really getting anywhere but where they started from.

Learn to be Still, a song by the Eagles, sums up our struggle to find our lost souls. "We are like sheep without a shepherd, we don't know how alone, so we wander around this desert, wind up following the wrong God home."

I find these words to be very profound in our efforts to break free from other's expectations and labeling of our individuality. Embrace them and let them take you to great heights of individual expression and creativity. Make your own path in this world by singing the words in your heart, painting the colors in your mind, and unleashing the feeling of free flight in your soul.

Some of us live in a world that only knows a structured expression of self. In this world your creativity will cease to grow. Claim your world for yourself now by believing in your gifts!

Reclaim your direction!

Unless we release the ties from a past that have bound us, we will continue to stir with an unsettled frame of mind that disrupts our natural harmony. With it comes the pain, confusion and emotions that lead us astray.

When you release the perils of your past, hold the moment you are living at present, and trust the unfolding of your future, that all is for the good. Let go of the fear, pain and resentment that has kept you grounded and stifled. With a freed mindset, you can dwell in a world without negativity. You can live in a world of goodness and positive action.
As you release all that was, celebrate your new life. Let the wind of today be the carrier of all that held you back.

In 1963, at age eight, I was able to write about this. This was long before I ever had to really practice it or pass it on as practical advice for others.

The brisk spring air blowing gently
Will pick you up and carry you away
To a far off place on another day.
You will stay there from now until then

And come back never, never again.

Then there will be no question in you or others of your existence and of your purpose. Those who do not see this will be bound to their own limitations. As they dwell in submission, you will be growing and prevailing in your beauty without restrictions.

"And it was the vision of God to create artists, musicians and writers whom with all their gifts combined would get the blind to see, the deaf to hear and the numb to feel."

"And you shall continue in that state of serenity without fear to unlock your own sense of peace, wellbeing and discovery, that which has kept you hidden for so long."

"Be not one to stay in the confines of others regression because you are a caring, loving soul. Care for and love those still as you soar."

"Cast away from our true self, we wander aimlessly, attracting those things and people in opposite reflection of our aspirations."

"You are an incredible person who sees extraordinary beauty in all. Let that beauty manifest and paint over the past to unveil a life of peace and harmony."

"The despairing world has dissipated. Bless the wind as those ashes are carried far from you."

"When we cling to all that was, we inhibit all that is and shall be. Let your inner beauty pour upon your canvas and rid the mask of all that has kept you hidden."

My dear friend, AFFIRM: "I am the leader of my life instead of the follower. If I feel lost in this moment, I shall trust in my Higher Power to lead me home again."

"Life is too precious to be defined by age."

The Spirit Of All Good Rises From Within The Soul

My dad and I went to church a few months back. He will be ninety-five years old in two weeks.

I sat next to him feeling a wave of appreciation run through me. I guess this was my Higher Power letting me know the true definition of happiness!

I didn't have to ask, it just washed over me.

I spent the next hour bathing in the wonderful memories of times my father and I shared.

Life has an uncanny way of presenting things to us when we least expect. It could be an opportunity that opens one door when another closes, it could be the discovery of a partner you've waited a lifetime to find, or it could be, as in my case, the realization that aging has a way of showing us how precious each moment in life is.

Today, I shared one hundred and twenty of those precious moments sitting next to a man that, only in recent years, have I come to allow myself to "let go and let God" show me just how special my Dad is.

I am blessed to be able to share a moment of giving thanks that I have him to love in person at this time in our lives. I learned something about him today – the spirit of good rises from within the soul.

As we were driving to the church my Dad looked over at me and said. "I go to church twice a week but I am not a religious man."

In the fifty-seven years I have been in his life and in the forty years I spent disagreeing with his view on the world, I have to humbly admit, this was the most profound statement he ever made to me! Those words sent a seismic scale shock that riddled right through me, shaking any negativity I ever held about this man out of every limb in my body.

That one statement instantly put perspective on every time I had asked myself why he is the way he is.

That one statement said it all, and in the process, answered many questions I had about my own shortcomings.

As I let what my Dad said filter through me, I began to understand that this man has been striving for most of his life to find answers within himself to the same questions I had been asking of him. The reason he couldn't change his ways that I constantly held against him, was because he had yet to know why himself.

So what my father was telling me with that one statement was that he sought God as his teacher and was now admitting to me his failure to either connect with or listen to Him.

How uncanny that I could see a crystal clear reflection in his eyes of myself in that moment.
I began to see the answer to that same question about my own inability, for many years, not to be able to see what I was not doing right in my own life. Mine, and my Dad's reason, for anything that did not work out, is simple.

We had called upon God, and God came to us and in our own times of seeking. We both had shaken our heads yes, as if to say we had understood, when we were merely just shaking our stubborn heads in a yes that had no true conviction attached to it.

When my father tells me he is not a religious man, I interpret what he is saying as this; he keeps trying but just can't seem to get it right. He feels he can't get it right because of how others react to his ways.

He is not living in an effort to live right by himself, but living in an effort to do right by what others think is right for them.

Confused? Please, don't be, let me clarify this.

When we live our life to please others, we neglect the life that our Higher Power has planned for us. Mind you, that power will never interfere with your stubbornness to listen, because it takes up too much time and energy. That power will merely let you go about your ways stumbling and falling until you look up from the ground and ask for a helping hand. Time after time, that hand will be there to lead and guide.

I have come to a point in my life where I accept and listen.

I am at a place where I know my direction is guided by something greater. I am who I am, and can lovingly accept that now. In seeing this in me, I see how easy it is to accept others. I believe there is good in all of us just waiting to surface.
If we want to live our lives pleasing others, we must first be pleased with ourselves.

I do not smile at you because I am trying to win you over, I smile because I am happy inside, and that is the expression I am naturally projecting. If in turn you smile back, perhaps I did invoke something in you, or maybe your inners are just as naturally happy.

I put my arm around my Dad at church, looked straight up at the ceiling and said, "Thanks."

This morning I pictured my dad in my mind, smiled and said "Thanks," again.

I will continue giving thanks, not to please him, but to remind myself just how precious a gift he is in my life.

This is where the good rises up from my soul and gets projected to all around me. This is where I can let go of all I used to feel

I had to try and change, and welcome acceptance of all for what it is.

This is how life is meant to be lived.

After forty years of trying to change my Dad, I realized it was me who needed to change.

Why not take a look at the people in your life today that you have fought against, disagreed with, turned your back on, and ask yourself one very important question. "Could it be me that has been the one needing to change all along?"

As we rush to judge, to give our opinions, to try and change, let it be that we now rush to see just who we are and how we can change.

In working with what goes on within us, instead of what goes on in the external world, we begin to be able to be honest and upfront with what we need to do to strengthen the good in our souls.

That inner goodness radiated outward is all we need to live right and treat others right.

In closing, I have to disagree with my Dad. I believe he is a man of conviction and belief.

I think my father is a lot like me.

We realized we are not perfect. We made some mistakes or wrong choices in life. We both wanted to be the best fathers, husbands, friends, coworkers and presence in our communities.

My Dad and I spent our lives trying to please others. We also spent many years living with the guilt of not living up to others expectations.

As I was telling my Dad, it is okay for him to let go of all those years of blaming himself; that he had been forgiven. I smiled to myself and realized I had just forgiven myself in the process.

My dear friend, AFFIRM: "Today I make amends with my parents no matter how I feel about my childhood. Let compassion guide me to the understanding that the ones who raised me did the best they could."

CHAPTER SIX

LETTING GO LETS US GROW

"Break free of the past and you will soar effortlessly to a new beginning."

Letting Go Lets Us Grow

Many of us have felt the need to let go, and many of us have been let go. Release of something, and being released from something, is a growing-up part of life.

Whether it's a baby having to let go of their pacifier, a small child kissing his or her mother goodbye and crying on their first day of school, a married couple realizing they must let go of one another after vowing to be together forever, or an elderly man or women standing at their beloved's grave site, life evolves and grows from letting go.

Letting go is never easy.

When you have grown accustomed to someone, it is very hard to see life without that person. When you enter a relationship, you do so with the hope that it will never end.

True love in relationships never dies, the love you shared holds memories to be cherished forever. In an ideal relationship these memories make you stronger and enable you to see time spent together as a stepping stone to a more enriching life filled with positive gifts.

These gifts come in many forms, but the most important gift of all is the one that you give to others by sharing the rewards from having shared love and friendship with someone for a time in your life that was special.

While it sometimes seems difficult to understand how one can give away the gifts of love they shared with someone else, we must try and understand that gifts of love are the circle of life that helps the world turn.

Love was never intended to be taken and tucked away so that it could never be felt by others. Love was meant to be universal so it could become eternal. With eternal love, the world and all life will grow with loving abundance.

By sharing we give unselfishly what has been given to us unselfishly. By giving unselfishly, we are able to receive those gifts of love to give to others.

We wish our relationships will leave us feeling a sense of completeness but life does have its ups and downs no matter how positive or optimistic our outlook may be. Sometimes we do have unfulfilling relationships.

Often one's feelings are kept hidden out of fear that the recourse that may come from conveying our truth will cause pain to the other.

In relationships, the bearer of truth often remains torn between conveying their innermost feelings and wrestling with holding on to someone that they no longer feel is right for them.

Day after day, as one holds back from expressing themselves honestly, this isolation of true feelings and emotions can cause resentment and anger to build up. Avoiding the issue is the worst way of handling the need to let go. This will eventually result in undue stress and anxiety.

The remedy, although it may pain and hurt, is a simple one.

No matter how much you care and feel love for the other, if you truly do not feel the desire to be in a relationship with that person anymore, the truth must be told. This is the greatest gift you can give yourself and the other person.

The emotions that follow, the pains of hurting or being hurt, are a natural part of letting go of someone we love, but they too shall pass, and in the long run, feelings of love and respect will prevail. And both will be able to move on to a better place of being, with themselves and in their life.

You may ask how one can get to a point of not loving someone you have loved for some time?

There are many factors that constitute this transition of feelings. People change, as does their life. Situations are altered, as are our mindsets. What worked last week, last month or last year, may not be working in the present.

When you no longer feel you can face life's challenges, when the road leads to nowhere and the future has become a cloud of obscurity, when you can't find that love that once kept you moving forward against all odds, it is time to step back and see just where that feeling may have come undone.

Taking the time to go within and seek the guidance of that greater power will reveal the truth in the right time.

As we allow ourselves this time and space, we are able to gain an understanding of why things aren't what they used to be.

Most of us, out of habit and familiarity, tend to cling to the things that were comfortable, often fighting change and the need to let go and redirect our lives. This reluctance merely holds up new opportunities from coming into our life.

Letting go and letting the unknown arrive is scary for most, but when you really think about your current state, what is the worst that could happen?

Letting go lets you welcome a whole new beginning, a bright light of change and challenge.

When we are accepting, we are welcoming, and when we welcome, the opportunities for a new life abound.

I was afraid for many years to let go of the things I had grown accustomed to, the all-too-familiar daily routines I felt were keeping me tucked safely under the arms of my protector and away from the claws of failure.

Denial mixed with feelings of misery and anger were my escape from the reality that I, no one else, was the one holding myself back. I did this out of complacency. All I was doing was settling and placing a low value on my life.

I finally woke up! In my awakening I took inventory of the things that had held me back. I did see fault in my being. I saw it and accepted it and set out to change my ways.

As I did this, my self-esteem and confidence began to escalate. All good in every area of my life began to show up. I did not have to seek or ask, I only had to believe that I was deserving of love in my life, and let my arms be opened to receive all this beautiful abundance.

I may not know you, but I know of you through my own experiences in this life. We are all here for the same purpose, and that is what I have come to know. That purpose is to love, to be loved, to be happy and live in the reality of our unfolding dreams that enables us to do something in this world we love, something that defines us as individuals, something that touches upon the hearts of everyone we encounter on this incredible journey, and gives them the light they need to be true to themselves.

My dear friend, AFFIRM: "Today I accept what I must do in order to live a life filled with love. I love myself first and know who I am. I accept no compromises, because in settling for anything less, I not only deprive myself of what I am entitled to, I deprive those I take into my life, out of fear."

"Wake up and smell the flowers."

Let Life Unfold In Color

I sat outside tonight thinking about our world and all those I know, past and present.

I thought about the people I had spoken to recently, processed their conversations through my mind bank and thought, "Damn, there is really a lot of complaining and misery going on around me!"

Sorry, my friends but I do not have time for that negativity in my life.

Do I have this right?

I certainly do and so do YOU!

You see, we all need to just sit and let life unfold in color right before our eyes!

There is a simple approach to a life void of all complaints.

Nature does not have room for anything more than beauty in its simplest form. Our world was created for enjoyment not destruction.

The mountains, the seas, the lands and all our people were put here merely to love, to embrace, to appreciate and savor.

The pains and miseries we can use to replace the beauty are an easy escape that ultimately gets us no place but locked into a world of dissatisfaction and non-appreciation of all that surrounds us in our every moment of being alive.

There is a saying, "Wake up and smell the flowers." WOW...when do you wake up and do just that?

When was the last time you actually took the time to open your eyes to the colors of this magnificent world?

When did you last set your alarm clock to greet the sunrise?

Can you recall the time you actually were in awe over the setting sun?

Simple...yes, simplicity does have a way of keeping us grounded in the present, in the now of our existence, when all else is faltering around us. There are so many things tugging at us daily to close our eyes, hearts and minds to the "whatever you believe" created beauty of life.

We have two choices; one choice is to bitch and complain and let our negativity take us way off course to a place that becomes an extreme struggle to find our way home, or, we can just accept what life has dealt us, see what we have, and come up with a divine approach to our existence.

By taking the time to see the true colors that surround us, by looking outward at all this earth is made of, and by coming to the realization that it truly is within ourselves to dispel all that we have been programmed to believe, have been besieged by the media to believe, and feel too weak to believe otherwise, we come to see things about ourselves that spell strength.

In this realization we rid ourselves of weakness.

I pray for all faced with a heart that is closed or has closed to love because of the misconception, whether it was inbred or acquired as a result of living with others who were blinded by insecurities, lack of self esteem and an attitude, that control of others is the only way to survive.

A strong statement, I know, but one that really comes out of compassion and love from my own experiences.

I feel and have compassion for all those I encounter everyday who continue living in a world that does not allow them to venture beyond the fear of their upbringing.

My dear friend, AFFIRM: "Today I let go and let the beauty of this world unfold before my eyes."

"Be willing to let go and let faith guide you to your next destination."

Renew Your Life By Forgiving

We often let go of someone or something in order to become a stronger and better person, so that we may be the best we can be for others. Quite often those we leave behind come to the realization they need to change as well, in order to move ahead. This is true of respecting another's need to be let go.

If you are in a relationship with someone you truly care about who feels the need to be let go, let them go! Do not hang on for fear of losing that person, because it will destroy the beautiful friendship that can be built upon the respect you have shown them by your decision to step aside.

In any relationship, whether it is one of love or friendship, there may come a time when feelings arise deep inside that tell us this is no longer right. By trusting those feelings you are showing not only acceptance and maturity, but self-confidence and love for thy self as well as respect for others feelings and needs.

You may not always see the love that awaits you through the fog you are in, in this moment of dissolve, but just as the sun is bound to burst through the cloud, so is that love. This comes from clarity, which evolves from being honest with ourselves.

Some people have a hard time letting go because they fear not knowing what awaits them. They cling and hang onto the familiar in an effort to avoid what they feel may disrupt a place of complacency.

When we become too ingrained in anything in our world, we set ourselves up for potential failure. I do not mean failure from the efforts we have exercised to secure our relationship or livelihood, but failure to prepare ourselves with the ability to adapt to change.

Change is inevitable! It happens every moment of our life. There is constant change and shifting going on, not only within us as we grow, but in our universe.

When our relationships begin to change, it is the result of one or both people realizing something, or seeing something about themselves they failed to notice in their complacent state of being. The same is true of a job and even our environment.

Successful people are able to see this change occurring. They have the faith and courage to accept these changes and they set out to rethink their position in any given situation.

In a relationship, the person who embraces any type of shift in themselves or their partner, can re-strategize or conclude what needs to be done either to maintain or dissolve that relationship.

Sometimes as much as it hurts to walk away, after weighing all other possible solutions, the outcome is evident that parting is the best solution.

Employees called in to be presented with the news that they are no longer needed, will feel an initial set of emotions: anger, disbelief, helplessness and resentment.

If you have not seen it yet, the movie, "Life as a House" starring Kevin Klein is a wonderful and heartwarming story of a man who is released from his job, is faced with more than he can handle, and turns what could be a reason to give up all hope, into the building of a lifelong dream. He came to a place of letting go and choose to accept all that was thrown at him as an opportunity to create a positive outcome.

I have a friend who recently walked away from her job after many years. She is one of the most dedicated, loving and caring persons I have ever met.

As our friendship began to blossom and she shared her life story, I saw that life had thrown her some pretty tough curves. I did not see her swinging and missing at what was thrown, what I saw was a person able to rise above great adversity and take control of the outcome.

Her ability to see all good in anything negative helped her to turn things around in her favor. Just as she has risen and built her own life as a house, she will use this experience as a motivational tool to even further beautify her dream.

Do not be afraid to walk away for the sake of your wellbeing. In the long run, what may appear at first an effort to tear you down, will emerge as the erection of new found dreams and renewal of all those caring and loving qualities that have helped you overcome life's obstacles all along.

Sometime we need to change our physical environment as well to let the doors of opportunity open to a new and refreshing start in a whole new place. This is the beauty of being able to let go and be open to all the boundless possibilities our wonderful world and its people have to offer.

A few years ago I addressed a room full of displaced workers. My speech was geared towards motivating them, opening up their eyes to new possibilities in spite of now being faced with a life altering event.

My message was a clear and simple one. It was based on the idea behind my favorite book, Jonathan Livingston Seagull, written by Richard Bach. I asked these senior executives to use their life's experiences as the wind beneath their wings to enable them to soar beyond mere definition.

Seagulls are known for being scavengers. They seem pretty much complacent just gliding to the nearest food source as opposed to soaring to great heights, unlimited and undaunted by preconceived definitions about them.

"Jonathan," I told them. "Now, there was a seagull that saw himself in a different light."

"This gull was an out of the box thinker, one willing to take a risk and redefine his life." I went on.

"By doing so, he exceeded the definition of what a seagull's life is to be."

"In his quest to soar to great heights, to touch the heavens, there was never the fear of falling, and when he did, he rose right up and took to the heavens once again."

"Each and every one of you is Jonathan."

"Each and every one of you is now being defined not by what you have done in your life but by where you now stand."

"You can either feel sorry for yourself or you can redefine yourselves."

"Let all the experiences you have gathered along your journey release you from your current fears of failing. Let what you have done in your lifetime become the source of a new definition of your life."

"Become a mentor to someone just starting out, write that book you have always dreamed of writing, take that long awaited journey or relocate to the place of your dreams. Whatever it is you choose to do, use the winds of the life you have lived to lift you above and beyond all preconceived odds about your ability to reinvent your life."
The New Jersey Professional Service Group (PSG) speech 1999

Don't be surprised if there is a knock on your door, a phone call, letter or email one day from that very person you mentored thanking you for helping them see the light.

My dear friend, AFFIRM: "I always walk away with a smile on my face and love in my heart for myself and others, no matter what transpires."

"Communicate with a loving voice and compromising heart."

The Right Way To Resolve Conflict

Sitting down to talk to your partner about financial problems, your children about behavioral issues, or your boss about a performance issue, are situations where we have the luxury of mapping out what we want to say beforehand.

As the saying goes, there is a time and a place for everything. If we recognize this and plan accordingly, things will most likely be resolved in an amicable and stress-free manner.

Our Higher Power, if we choose to listen, will help us with the answers, in the right time and the right place.

If we try to make things happen and take an, "I want it resolved now" approach, we have already set the table for failure.

The effort to find resolution will turn into conflict, which then brings us back to having to face another round of conflict resolution.

By letting go and letting God, we allow ourselves the luxury of calming.

As we begin to ease our minds, our bodies release the negative emotions associated with confrontation and we actually gain focus and clarity.

This is our inner peace driving us now.

Relax, sit back and enjoy the scenery. Trust the timing of your Higher Power. This is not designed to keep you in suspense; it is given to create harmony and resolution in all dealings where negative emotions, if allowed to prevail, will be certain to cause an uncomfortable feeling.

During this time out, ask yourself two simple questions.

1. "What is my best approach to present my side of the story?" This allows us time to stop and think before we react hastily. We can review our options and in many cases we will wind up presenting a recommendation that is agreeable and workable for all involved.
The next step will give you better insight and understanding of the other person.

2. "Have I taken the time to understand where the other person is coming from?"
Quite often we meet resistance when we fail to take into consideration pre-existing conditions that may affect the other person's cooperation.

We never know what may have occurred seconds before we walked in the room, something that could ultimately affect the other's ability to be open and willingly engage us in constructive problem solving. You may want to, if you are not good at reading body language, politely ask if this is a good time to meet. And please, always respect if it is not, or you will put yourself back in that conflict resolution turnstile again.

In the long run, paying attention to what goes on around us, listening to our inner voice, knowing when to present something, and letting it rest in a power greater than us, will keep us from asking ourselves where we went wrong.

And believe me, your soul will be a happy camper taking this new approach.

My dear friend, AFFIRM: "Today I will make every effort to be a more loving, open and understanding communicator. With this approach and openness I can use love to resolve and pave the way for positive resolution in any conflicting situation."

"Eliminate the obstacles standing in the way of your dreams."

Things Happen For A Purpose

I ask you to think back to any situation in your life when you wanted it, "NOW!"

In this mindset, we have a tendency to try to control the outcome of something.

Control is really our EGO in disguise, playing against the rules of right circumstance. This is all part of our persona creeping in to take over the right energy, replacing it with an energy that tells us, WE are in charge our lives.

This is so far from the truth!

By accepting the natural processing of events, we are telling our egotistical mindset to take a hike!

By trusting in our Higher Power to guide the outcome, we are letting our self, the un-ego self, to get ready in whatever way needed to welcome the unfolding of the divine purpose in store for us.

As unique as we are as individuals, so are the events and outcomes. They are designed uniquely for each of us. What may work for someone else, may not work for you.

If you have a dream in your heart to follow and someone tells you it is not right for you, what they are really saying is that the same dream was not right for them, or, in many circumstances, they allowed someone else to convince them this dream was not for them.

When another person tries to hold you back or makes you feel that you are not worthy of what you believe in your heart, this is a reflection of their insecurities.

Follow your dream with a heartfelt conviction guided by your Higher Power. You will find you are able to rise above any obstacles that could stand in your way and embrace them as motivators to set your sights higher.

How do you know if your dream is real?

When you live it, does your heart open up and cleanse you with emotions?

Are you able to see it unfolding even in darkness?

Are you able to sustain it when statistics say you need to walk away?

Dreams are something we develop as a child and grow as we grow.

Sometimes it seems we have lived a great portion of our lives putting our dreams aside when, in reality, we were not ready to see them through.

By letting go and trusting in the process, by keeping that dream always on your path no matter where life takes you, it will never be lost. When it unfolds, you will be ready to run with it!

We may not always see the true purpose unfolding, because our nature is to allow our anxiety to force that unfolding instead of letting go. Trust in the outcome and know it will come for all the right reasons in its own time.

The ego is really a reflection of weaknesses that results in an infliction of those weaknesses upon others when the ego is allowed to take over.

My dear friend, AFFIRM: "In this moment I stop trying to control the outcome. I believe in my heart that when I willingly let go and let God, all will work out for the best for myself and all else concerned."

"Tough love is the mender of all."

Love Has To Be Tough Sometimes

When you truly love someone there grows a unique understanding that allows one to give without question to another in need.

The one we love, we appreciate not for what they do for us all the time, but what they do for others. Loving someone for this characteristic is an unselfish portrayal of love as well as a sign of security and growth.

For those who have felt a ping of hurt, perhaps jealousy or envy, when we saw someone we love giving to another, this came out of a feeling of insecurity which comes from lack of self love.

Being able to love yourself comes from loving others without expecting anything more than respect in return, and simply being able to be alone in peace and harmony without feeling the need to invite another into your space to create those feelings for you.

You will know you have come to this place of loving someone when you feel in your heart and in your every day existence that you can let go of the other with encouragement and goodwill, not with resentment or a feeling of being abandoned.

Only then will you be able to see that you have learned not only how to love but what true love really means.

This growth takes time and the willingness to look and address any issues surrounding your relationship.

If those issues relate to feelings of anxiety and disharmony, accusations and mistrust, this is not a healthy love and you are not seeing and or accepting the truth about yourself when it comes to loving another.

Remember, love creates harmony, not discord, in our lives.

When we can actually feel good about the love we have for ourselves enough that we no longer expect another to fill our needs, we are free in mind and spirit to love others. This too will allow the right feelings of love to come back to us.

Ask yourself, how can I say "I love you" to someone when I cannot allow myself to feel trust in them?

And, do you find yourself always putting the reasons for this lack of trust back onto the other person?

Let me open your eyes here for a moment!

When we find ourselves pushing off our own feelings onto anyone or anything outside of us, we are failing to see and accept deep-rooted causes for our actions.

A person who lives with jealousy of another is a person who has either experienced unfaithfulness in their life through a previous relationship, or is the one who has or is living unfaithfully.

A person who lives with insecurities is one who has either been brought to feel they are not worthy, or relies on a crutch to hide their true being.

An addiction is an escape from reality, a denial of facing ones responsibility to deal with whatever it was, or is, going on in their life.

This is self-burial of our God existence for living a happy, serene and prosperous life.

Once we are able to accept our denial and face the truth about how and why we are living precariously, inducing pain and misery into our existence through false highs, the covers begin to shed, the truth comes unlocked and we are able to understand why we have sacrificed good living.

With right living comes right loving.

We may not be able to do this all by ourselves, but in essence it must come from self in order to be recognized and faced.

Coming from the heart of the one who is living the lies of existence is the only place the truth will emerge.

While we all need love and support as we embark upon our new life, the pains and reality of how we have lived, or are living, must be looked at alone.

By shouldering the weight and responsibility of our actions, only then will we begin to build upon the strength that eventually will enable us to walk free of the crutches that have become our way of life.

And, for those who love you, being there to save you every time you fall, denies you the true meaning of love.
Tough love does not say a person no longer cares, in fact, it is quite the opposite.

By taking a firm stand and letting the one we love go to face the consequences of their actions merely says our love is there to help them rebuild their life, if that in fact is what they choose to do.

By letting go, we allow the one we love to see, to think, to act for and grow for his or herself.

As parents, spouses, partners or friends, the decision to put a person's life, whom we love, back in their own hands, is a tough love decision.

Once it is made, we must honor our word, if we do not, we fail in our love for that person.

Remember, only when you are left to face what you have put in front of you, only then will you see clearly just what you have to do to come out a stronger and better person.

Tough love has let me go, and I have had to let go out of tough love, but in either circumstance, I have grown. And as you will see in your own time, you will grow and be thankful to the one who gave you no choice but to figure life out for yourself.

And, for the one you let go, if they are true to themselves about living life right, they will grow and be thankful to you for cutting the cords of codependency.

As loving, caring souls, we know it is the will and way of our Higher Power and right way of living to be of service and help those in need.
That service comes from a love that does not seek to enable but to free.

For it is in the freedom we give another out of love, we too let them learn to spread their wings and fly.

My dear friend, AFFIRM: "Today I accept responsibility for my actions. In doing so, I will not have reason for having to say I am sorry later on."

CHAPTER SEVEN

FINDING THE CHILD IN YOU

"Bring the child out in you and have fun with life today."

Finding The Child In Me Once Again

I went to the beach last night, and listened without constraint to the calming sound of the waves touching the shore. As the moon's light filtered through the night and reflected her rays upon its incredible vastness, I knew I was exactly where I was supposed to be in that moment.

Was it fate that had taken me to this place in this time, or was it a higher calling leading me?

I didn't wait for an answer, I just accepted the moment as a reminder of who I once was. I held it as a gift I had locked away many years ago, yet held its memories in my heart through all that had passed my way since then.

It had been so long since I let the beauty of this world touch my heart that way. In that moment, I knew it was the time for me to feel it as I had known it so long ago. My life had come as it was supposed to, full circle. It did in that very moment because I was ready to embrace it. Only now, I had a lifetime of knowing and knew just how to receive it.

That longing fell upon me like the mist that caressed my face from the cresting waves.

As the evening's light bounced upon the sea and scattered beneath the cresting waters, an almost eerie illumination filled each breaker with the shadows of a spirit bathing. It was as if God was washing His soul at the water's edge.

And onto the warm sands where I stood, that pureness pushed forth and touched the flesh of my bared feet. As the cleansing from the waters trickled up through me, I began to feel as though I was slowly being draped in a shroud of wholeness woven from the heavens. My heart was aglow with a feeling that I knew and loved as a child.

As a child, I believed the beauty in this world was something that never, ever goes away, that my heart could never hurt and my soul would always be filled with light. For so long I held onto that, and for even longer, I seemed to let it go.

I began to walk with my thoughts and with each step I took, that child I once knew walked beside me.

I looked down at this beautiful child and smiled. Oh that laughter and innocence coming from him was so much how I wanted to be again.

I walked on into the night holding that little boy by the hand, remembering all that I had been. And, as if I were in a dream, my hand was suddenly empty.

Then it came to me. I wasn't in a dream. I was seeing me as a child. And in that moment I realized, I never left behind what I grew up believing.

As I stood by the waters' edge and felt what I was feeling, I knew I was seeing the beauty I saw as a child again. I knew I believed in what I believed as a child again. And I knew I had come full circle from all I believed as a child, to where I now belonged as a man.

My dear friend, AFFIRM: "Today I learn to live and embrace daily my childlike view of life. I skip circled stones across the water, jump in a puddle, make a snowman, touch the petals on a flower and laugh, just to bring a smile to my heart."

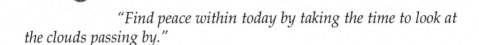

"Find peace within today by taking the time to look at the clouds passing by."

Clouds, Natures Greatest Remedy for Stress

<u>*Clouds, Just White, Fluffy Clouds*</u>

I stand
I stare upwards mesmerized by what is to unfold.
Slowly evolving, quickly churning with the wind
The art of each cloud appears in formation.
Enhanced by the setting sun
All the wonderment of the universal forces
Unveils itself in an exploding paradise for all eyes to see.
And yet, so few of these eyes ever touch upon this unfolding beauty.
– 9/12/2011

As a child I felt great peace lying in an open field just gazing upwards at the sky's art. This is one of life's simplest pleasures and tools for enriching our imagination.

Our hurried world has kept us looking straight ahead as the heaven's canvas recreates and defies conformity. Ah, we should all have such a wondrous freedom to expand, as does a cloud, beyond our self-imposed boundaries.

Today, we can easily be mesmerized without artificial stimulation as a result of all the imagery propped up in front of us.

Time of creativity and inventiveness is often left to artificial dissemination and application. Once it leaves the real and natural mind of the applicator, it gets filtered through an electronic circuit board of imagery and programming.

While I may seem to contradict myself at this point I have to confess, as a writer and publisher, I would not want to do without these software tools and electronic gadgets.

Yet, I am grateful for the time I spent as a child, and the time I still spend today lying on my back gazing upwards at the artwork of the universe. In all my consumption of electronic stimuli, I still stimulate and nourish my growth by feeding on nature's beauty.

When your hurried life offers you a moment of quiet and solitude, take the time to get to know who you really are.

Clouds, stars, sunrises and sunsets, mountaintops, vast horizons, desert sands and lush valleys all are of my expressionism when it comes to writing and painting.

Make our natural world part of your day today!

Whether you live atop a mountain overlooking a lush valley, enjoy the dawning or dusk of another day from your front yard, or find yourself walking through the concrete mazes of city life, the sky will always be above you wherever you may go.

Take the time to get to know who YOU are on this day. You will be pleasantly surprised at how your mind becomes an expanse of nature's beauty.

Our everyday caterings to living up to the obligations and responsibilities imposed upon us by work, family and daily dealings, will drain us of our ability to think clearly.

Often we find ourselves as intellectually sharp and focused as we may normally be, entangled in stress. The overbearing pressures of obligations that cause our minds to become overloaded as we rush to meet deadlines, cram for school, get caught under the tow of child rearing and meeting family needs, fighting the emotional drains of strained and trying relationships on various levels, become mazes of mental disorientation caused by mind circuitry overloads.

These overloads need diffusion.

A peaceful and serene mind is clear of obstruction. It is capable of helping us to lead a life of good health filled with focus and clarity. As we apply this to our daily living, we create a balance that enables us to sort out and remedy everyday obstacles. Our tasks transcend from laborious chores to challenges. We welcome these challenges as tools for growth and stimulation. And to think, all of this chaos was sedated by the passing of clouds, just white, fluffy clouds.

My dear friend, AFFIRM: "Today I will stop the world, get off, and savor the beauty of this incredible world I live in."

"We all go through tough times in life that test us, not for weakness, but strength."

Creating Boundaries Defines Self-Love

It takes a strong person to forego the strength of ego that keeps them living in a weakened state of falsehood. It takes an even greater strength to see the truth and humbly ask their Higher Power to intervene and lead the way.

Once you take hold of this and make it your daily practice, you will begin to lead a fulfilling and happy life. With this you will feel inner peace, self-acceptance, happiness and contentment. Most importantly you will know and feel self-love.

As we begin to love ourselves, we start to attract only those people and things into our lives that are a reflection of us.

As we gain a deeper understanding of ourselves, we are able to define and establish boundaries. These boundaries protect us and keep us moving forward on our new path of self-love, self-awareness, self-respect and enlightenment.

If we continue to allow our life to be driven by the will of others, we will surely suffer from lack of self-worth. We will find ourselves lacking self-esteem, getting caught in a rut of purposelessness, and lacking the desire and motivation to do anything about it. Our love of self replaces the need to look for others to fill that love. We can now look to others to compliment, not satisfy, this love for us.

Successful relationships between adults, parents and children, friends and even coworkers, are built upon and driven by respect, praise and love. These traits are motivators and positive re-enforcers that say, "I trust you, accept you without judgment and love you as you are."

As we walk on this "new me" path, one surrounded by people and things that motivate us, we know that too many hours of our time have been invested and we have had to learn many lessons and endure many setbacks to continue living against our grain.

Our awakening tells us we no longer have to spend our energy trying to fit in or concede to anything that just doesn't feel right in our heart. This way of life lets you move forward without that old, haunting feeling you are not good enough.

With our love of self, we now know we do not have to convince ourselves or others to accept anything more about us than the "face value" of who we are.

Living in truth, with integrity and for the respect of all, does give one the right to establish boundaries than can no longer be infiltrated by another's ill will. We all go through tough times in life that test us not for weakness but strength.

The most successful people in life got there because they had everything stripped away, and redirected their lives by letting go and accepting responsibility for all the actions and choices that caused their demise. In doing this spiritual cleansing and self-realization, new success was even greater and held more permanence in every aspect of their lives.

Whatever makes us sing in life is our choice. Let our song carry a message of love, hope, respect and caring, for all.

My dear friend, AFFIRM: "My love of self establishes boundaries that will not allow my values, morals and will, to be trespassed against. I know I am entitled to say "NO" when my heart tells me something is not right for me!"

CHAPTER EIGHT

CHILDREN ARE OUR

MOST PRECIOUS GIFTS

"From the moment a child's eyes open, the world they see belongs to them."

Children Are Our Most Precious Gift

When any child is encouraged, loved and given the freedom to explore and uncover our world in their own way, what they unfold in their lifetime will greatly enhance the lives of all they encounter on their journey of discovery.

Let a child discover what they were put on this earth to do and the world will be a better place as a result of that child's ability to see and feel things through the heart and mind of innocence.

As parents we always want the best for our children.

Often we will try to direct them and protect them from the experiences we had to learn from when we were growing.

Too often we, as parents and guardians, become over protective out of our own fears. The fears we use to protect our children are the result of the falls we took and the mistakes we made in our own lives.

The reason we held onto those fears is simple; our parents or the guardians of our upbringing were always there to remind us of their own past, their own falls and mistakes, not knowing their constant reminders were holding us back from discovering the world in which we needed to grow in our own right.

As a result, we grew in the fear mindset of our parents, unable to let our children go and grow, overprotecting in an effort to prevent them from experiencing life on their own.

It doesn't matter how old or young your children are in this moment, you can still make amends and release them to become themselves.

Can you do this?

First you need to release yourself from your own fears of your past upbringing. Once you are able to do this, you will be able to let your children go. I do not mean this in a physical sense but in an emotional one.

Emotions play a major part in growing our fears.

When I was a little boy, my grandmother would take me outdoors with some pieces of bread in a brown paper bag. We would stand at the edge of the grass and begin to sprinkle the bread across the lawn. It has never ceased to amaze me the divine connection between something as simple as a piece of week old bread and God's animal kingdom.

My "Yayee," as I affectionately called her, would then take me by the hand and walk over to the large oak tree at the corner of her backyard. We would sit there on a blanket where she would read to me as the birds and squirrels began to flock harmoniously to the bread.

We sat there for hours creating these peaceful, loving memories of my childhood.

I grew up in a world that understood peace, beauty, serenity and appreciation for nature. Find this within you and use it as your guide in raising your children. If it seems difficult to see this within you, it is because you have not let go of the pains of your own upbringing. In order to grow, you must be willing to let go of all that has held you back from moving forward.

In 1982, eight years before my first child was born, I began to write thoughts about a gift I knew would come to me when I was ready to know just how precious it was.

That gift came into my world in 1990.

Two years later I was blessed with the gift of a daughter.

My children are now grown and have begun to make their way in this world.

Both of them have now set out to seek their own dreams.

As I reflect upon the years and all the trying times and experiences it took for them to get where they are now in life, one moment comes back that has made me smile all those years.

I see the first moment they opened their eyes to this world and saw it was theirs to discover in their own way, in their own time and with their own gifts.

They have done just that.

As we are there to love and help guide our children through their lives, if we do so with love and encouragement and not fear and threat, we raise children who are filled with love and a caring attitude for all forms of life.

If we allow them to discover through this love and encouragement, our children will always find their way back from any detours they may undertake in order to discover what it is they do and what it is they don't want for themselves in this world.

"It is our inherent nature to always find our way back to the brightest and most loving light and to run far from darkness."
6/30/2012

The following poems were written between 1972 and 1993.

The Dream

As the waves gently caress the sand in its liquid bare feet
I look at you lying so peacefully in my arms.
Born to me in a dream
Now
A reality.
As the moon casts its light upon the horizon
Turning the sky into a blazing heaven of gold
I pull you close to me, and watch as you drift off to sleep.
Close your eyes my child and dream
Of something as beautiful.
   –   1990

Every Day (Let your child discover the ocean)

Every day in our lives is a new beginning
To be written in the book of our dreams.
As oceans touch the shore, a new wave is born.
In its wake are many beautiful memories
Washed upon the sands.
Reach down and take them in your hands
They are the dreams of your every day
Don't ever let them be washed away.
 – 1972

Growing

Take the time in your life my child, and listen
To the wonderful sounds of the natural world
That surrounds you.
Open your heart to a song of beauty.
Climb a mountain
Love all of the world's little creatures.
The wind will be with you to guide your life
It will keep you strong throughout your flight.
As you begin to discover your true self
Reach for the sky.
Always live your life with honesty and compassion
Knowing my loving spirit will always be by your side.
– 1982

Parents

You spend your days watching your children grow
You feel the pains of their tears
And the happiness of all their joys.
Though little time is spent listening to the ocean
The sound of the waves is clear in your mind.
A day comes when you look back upon the memories
Pausing, you shed a tear,
Not for the pains and joys of raising a child
But for the child that has grown.
– 1975

Mom

All through my life I have been building my own dreams
You have been there every step of the way.
Had it not been for the love and guidance you gave
I would have never been able to see the real beauty
In something as simple as a red rose

Or appreciating the respect others give me
For having good manners
Or being able to say I am sorry and admit when I was wrong.
– 1980

Accepting

Let me look into their eyes when they do wrong and see
The innocence of growing.
Let me reach out to hold them when they cry
Instead of pushing them away and telling them to be strong.
Let me listen to their harsh words when they are confused
And soothe them with kind words and love.
Let me turn my own weaknesses away from them
And show them my strength instead.
Let me see that they want the very best for me
As I want for them.
Let me stop and listen
And learn from them
For they are the true teachers of this world.
They are, our children.
– 1993

My dear friend, AFFIRM: "Today, no matter how old or young my children are in this moment, I can still make amends."

"*The gift of a child is one to be opened with the heart.*"

Loving Your Children Unconditionally

For all the parents who have given up their life for their children, you are the true definition of an angel's reflection of what God intended when he brought us into this world.

Having the gift of a child is one to be opened with a heart that pours out the warmth from the sun, and nursed with love that shines from the heavens above.

If we spend our life raising our children with the feeling that they will always find an open door, no time or distance will ever keep them too far for too long.

When we open our hearts to our children from the time they open their eyes to greet the world, we open their heart to a love that will always remain true no matter what happens in life.

Taking the time from our life to offer a shoulder to lean on, and an open mind to listen without opinion at any time of day or night, assures us we will never be alone.

At the start of each day, before the world beckons and pulls at your emotions and will, give your children a hug and tell them you love them. Your day will be filled with a tireless energy driven by that one moment you stopped to show you care.

When a child grows and can approach with patience and grace the troubles they face during the day, it is because you showed them compassion instead of anger when they forgot to do something, fell and tore up their new jeans, or didn't get perfect grades in school.

By laughing as we share stories of the stupid things we did growing up, our kids grow knowing it is okay to laugh at their own mistakes. And, they will be great storytellers.

Embracing your child with love and compassion when they come to you to share what they have done they feel is wrong, teaches them to be open and honest. They in turn will grow with honesty and integrity.

When we let our children see our emotions as a way of positive release, they too will be able to let their emotions be a natural part of life.

When we love our children unconditionally, we will be able to love all the same way.

If you feel you have pushed your child away, it is never too late to rekindle that love. Remember, children are resilient no matter how old they get, they can easily forgive with a warm hug, and an "I love you."

Go on, don't be stubborn, make that call and reconcile, you are still that child you were born to be...a reflection of God's love.

My dear friend, AFFRIM: "Today I spend time listening to a child's needs. I will build trust in them by showing I care about what goes on in their life."

"Today take time to remember all the good times from your childhood."

Paving The Way For A Healthy Childhood

Relationships come to us through circumstance, coincidence, fate, destiny, events or situations. These bonds of love and friendship are fostered throughout our lives by the influences of our upbringing.

Some begin as children and are carried with us well into our adulthood.

For many, these relationships unfold as young babies or adolescents, through meetings in an innocent setting left untouched by anything more than the gleeful quest to explore and discover the mysteries of life, as it blossoms with the change of the seasons.

The children are guided by a spiritually infused wide-eyed wonder, as the purity of emotions unfolds and are exchanged and shared willingly, and without expectations of anything more in return than to remember to hold the other dear to heart until the day we die. Ah, the wonder and beauty of being a child.

As the child grows and becomes part of a larger scaled socio-environment, acceptance now becomes a much more intricate measure of preconditioned adult expectations and influence.

The personality of that child, one that has confidently been growing and developing in a simplistic world of social interaction, now steps into a world of adult enacted rules and directives. This is the end of the innocence and the beginning of judgment, both by others and of self.

The birthright of a child, the gift of innocence and purity, is now being cast into the waters of social acceptance. The mind of that young heart hearing opinions of what is and what isn't right for him or her, now finds themselves seeking just what it will take to fit in. In this process all innocence becomes a scramble to redefine self.

As the child looks to be a part of the whole they find the welcome mat being pulled out from under them.

Criteria is created to measure all a child is, for the sole purpose of erasing a free thinking mind, and replacing it with guidelines for success in a world a child should not be expected to even think about during these vital development stages of life.

Children begin to be divided into classes, measured and scaled by aptitude and financial status.

Natural talent is overlooked for grade point averages and national test scores. No longer does it matter what the child thinks or dreams, what matters is the child's ability to prove themselves worthy of fitting in to a gradient of test percentiles.

Some children, the ones I deem gifted, know from the time they are a child, that pursuing their dreams is the way God intended. They have a spirit that guides them away from conformity to a world of unlimited possibilities.

The naysayers call these little wonders lost souls, who travel to the beat of a different drummer. I see them as God's brightest light.

I am one of those who listened to the sounds of my own music.

I began knowing this at a very early age.

Like many, I allowed myself to be swept up in other's expectations and definitions of what was right and wrong for me. I succumbed to the pressure.

At points in my journey I stopped, questioned, began heading in the direction of my dreams, but then I found myself stepping right back on to the freeway of life going with the flow of what I was expected to do.

Today, I am taking the time to define all I gave up.

I am learning everyday that relationships can be paved on endless highways.

I am reclaiming and moving each day, in each moment given, the course mapped from my wonder years.

Remember, relationships are constantly coming towards us. A clear vision of the road we currently travel invites boundless opportunities.

As I am self-injecting what I need to recapture what I want in this world to live and love right, I am using the gifts I know were given to me at birth.

I know now by letting go and accepting my parents for who they were, I accept the gifts of nurturing and love given to me in whatever time they had available, and even though I didn't always agree with them, they gave to me as best as they could in their own way.

My dear friend, AFFIRM: "Today I honor my parents and let go of any resentments and anger I have held. I know that they did the best they could. I take any lessons I learned and do things right by my own children."

"Children do not need to be labeled as adults."

Where Has Our Childhood Gone?

As a kid I was one hyped-out little son-of-a-gun.

You couldn't keep me still for one minute. I was like Forest Gump, always running from one place to the next.

I was talkative as hell, probably annoying with all the questions I asked.

You couldn't get me to sit longer than 10 minutes for any meal.

Heck, I played outside before school, at lunchtime, after school, after dinner until it was dark or time to go to bed.

Next day the cycle started all over again. Weather could have been rain, snow, hot, cold, it didn't matter; I was out there burning off that natural kid energy.

Was I being a kid, or did I have too much energy to be considered normal?

I managed the children's mentoring programs for elementary and middle school aged children and met many kids just like me.

These kids had much the same issues I had growing up; divorcing parents, one-parent households, younger or older siblings, and a whole lot of the same kid energy I had at their age.

I know times have changed and the age of the innocence has all but ended. I ask myself, "Why does the end of the innocence have to come before puberty?"

Fifty years ago, I was allowed to grow up experiencing the joys of being a child. There were no locked gates around our schoolyards. The only fences were the ones we swung for when we were at bat.

The only guns we brought to school were when we were dressed up as cowboys or policemen for our Halloween parade.

You either rode the bus, your bike, or walked with the kids in your neighborhood. There was no thirty-minute drop off and pick up lines of cars waiting to escort us safely to school and then home; we got there in one piece on our own.

We didn't have cell phones to text on, only a dime to make a phone call from the nearest phone booth, letting someone at home know we were going to be late for dinner and why.

If we were going over a friend's house after school, or had extracurricular activities like sports practice, the yearbook club, or rehearsal for the school play, keeping us after the last bell rang for dismissal; it was marked on the calendar hanging from the refrigerator.

Even if we had to stay for detention or got suspended (because we did act like smart alecks sometimes and defy authority in our own innocent ways), we weren't taken to the police station for questioning, our parents were summoned to come and get us and told why we were in trouble.

This was almost always dealt with by being grounded, no dates or friends over the house, no phone or television, and a week or two worth of chores.

For us this was like facing the firing squad!

We had cliques, not gangs. The only matching outfits we wore did not symbolize violence, it was a show of our school colors and spirit.

We had fire drills, not lockdowns.

We pulled fire alarms thirty minutes before school was over as a stupid prank to get an early dismissal.

The only metal that would have gone off, had we had metal detectors, was from the lunch boxes we carried.

We didn't have to walk into our schools and mow people down to show our anger over the state of the world, or to emulate some movie we had seen the previous weekend. We came home and mowed our lawns as part of our responsibilities.

We took out the trash, instead of speaking it and treating others like garbage.

We used our garages for band practice or to work on our cars, not to make deadly explosives in.
Our energy levels were high as a result of wanting to make a change for the good in our world, not for destructing it.

We had school nurses to take our temperatures and send us home if we were sick, not psychologists and psychiatrists to evaluate our mental wellness, and prescribe the latest trending med for hyperactivity if we were filled with natural kid energy, or anti-depressants if we were shy and quiet.

Today our children are being assessed as early as kindergarten to determine just where they fit in on the "potential to become a menace to society" flow chart.

If there is any indication in the classroom a child is disruptive because he or she is not able to sit still in one place for thirty-five minutes, this is not being diagnosed as normal behavior for adolescents.

The term attention deficit has replaced "just too young to focus for long periods of time."

The term bipolar has replaced, "I know he or she is moody, it's all part of growing pains."

Unfortunately many young children today are not being allowed to grow and develop normally because one bad apple had to spoil the bunch.

I understand there are children who do have issues of instability that require special attention.

I am aware that these children have root causes for their behaviors, but medicating them instead of getting to the root of the problem can be compared to an adult self-medicating on alcohol, illegal stimulants, or prescription drugs, to escape and cover up the realities of their problems.
I had some issues growing up.

My parents divorced when I was five. I moved quite a bit and I wasn't even an army brat. The friends I made I couldn't keep for long, because my bags were never really unpacked for too long before we were moving again.

I attended three different high schools.

I had an unstable and shaky upbringing, but I managed to get through it all.

As I read stories of preschool, kindergarten and elementary school aged children being prescribed drugs to alter their natural developing process, I am appalled. I am also thankful.

My thankfulness comes in knowing that the type of behavior I displayed as a young child was categorized as normal behavior for someone my age.

Adversity is something we all face in life. It can come at any age in many ways. The trauma children go through today as a result of family issues, such as separation, divorce, abuse, neglect, abandonment, poverty and death, is going to affect them at school.

Understand that the school environment for most kids is where they learn to socially interact and seek to be accepted outside of the home.

Naturally, if there are problems in the household, a child will look for a safe haven in his or her classroom.

A child will do what they need in order to get attention that is lacking elsewhere.

As a teacher, I hope you have been educated properly to be aware of and recognize changes in a child's behavior.

Understand first, that children today are under greater pressure than ever before in the classroom to achieve high marks, in order to remain competitive at every level of their schooling, from elementary, to middle and secondary grades, all the way up to college and post graduate levels of education.

Just as you are under the microscopic eyes of achievement in order to succeed as an educator, your students face the same scrutiny in their quest to achieve in the classroom.

I am not arguing that there may be a justifiable reason to summon the assistance of a Guidance Counselor or school therapist to help a child deal with personal issues; I do not believe a quick solution to the problem comes from writing a prescription.

As I sat here writing this, I thought about the conversation I had with a women my age today.

She is involved with kids as a Behavioral Therapist.

She planted the seed for this story by presenting me with her views on children who are being medicated so quickly today.

Asking my view, she commented. "I can't fathom how, if we continue to raise our children on medications that are altering the normal progression of childhood behaviors, they will, by the time they reach adulthood, be able to make any decisions for themselves."

I responded. "Isn't it time we start letting our kids be kids again?"

My dear friend, AFFIRM: "Today I will be a voice for the children of our world, as well as a listener."

"It is so important a child is nurtured with love and injected with praise from birth."

Coming From A Broken Home

Many children today come from broken homes, but that should not become the child's fault.

My children grew up in a divorced household, yet each of them in their own time made a decision to embrace their dreams in life and pursue them. This came from knowing that no matter what life's circumstances presented, they always knew they had my love and encouragement no matter what transpired in the marriage.

As parents, our relationships with our partners may not work out as planned, but that does not mean our children can't be given the loving resources and guidance they need to be successful in their own relationships.

A child who is given this will be able to welcome others into their life with open arms, respect, and love, instead of with anger and resentment.

A child who grows out of love and encouragement is a child who grows to give of that love unconditionally. Children growing up this way will feel confident in themselves enough to follow their own heart when it comes to the pursuit of dreams and relationships with others.

If you are at a stage in your life where you are reflecting upon the failure of your own relationships, instead of looking back in blame of all that was, look instead to now and all that can be.

Once you allow yourself to accept the things you cannot change and pour your energy into the things you can, you will begin to develop that lost child into a strong, healthy, self-confident and loving adult.

Develop a healthy and loving relationship now. Here are some things to practice:

Let go of the anger and resentment. This is the reason you are attracting others living with feelings of anger and resentment into your life, or pushing healthy, loving people away.

Define who you really are, what your dreams are, and what you want from life for YOU. This will allow you to grow, mature and stop seeking others to define who you are, and what you want from life.

Stop putting the blame and responsibility for the outcome of your present situation into the hands of someone else. This allows you to become independent, build self-esteem and assume responsible for your own decisions and the outcome of them.

Let go of the people you blame, so that they can let go as well of what transpired in their life, and move on to their own healthy and loving relationships, as you allow yourself to move on to yours.

Seek ways to fix your life on your own. This will help develop your dreams and passions for the life you want to lead.

All people in healthy, long term relationships are together in love, yet remain individuals in what defines them. When we attach all of our self to another, we drain them of their individuality and self-definition.

Be honest and upfront with all, it is the only way to build healthy relationships and to determine if the other is the right fit for you. If you want to make a good first impression, make it an honest one. If the other person can't accept your honesty, they cannot accept you! This is a good thing. It saves a lot of wasted time and heartache down the road.

Take this writing my friends and build a life for yourself of healthy relationships starting now!

My dear friend, AFFIRM: "I love and praise any children – babies, adolescents, teens or adults – in my life, at every chance I have. I remember that we all continue to grow no matter how young or old we are!"

"Children need to be allowed to be children."

Spending Quality Time With Your Children

Many of us have grown into adulthood lacking the security of a well-rounded family environment.

In today's society the family, as it was known through the innocent portrayals in television shows, has been decapitated by the constraints placed on the mother and father to provide financially for their children.

The days of a one person income that was sufficient enough to sustain all the expenses needed in providing food, shelter and education, have escalated at such astonishing costs, the one person earner in a medium income earning job no longer is able to provide all that is needed to bring home enough bacon to take care of their family's needs.

Yes, it is a sad situation which by today's economic downturn, massive layoffs as a result of escalating operating costs, jobs shipped overseas, the rising cost to provide health care, and, as positive as it may seem, the longer life expectancy of our senior population; a mother (or even by today's definition of a parent raising a child) or a father, are forced to leave the upbringing of their children in pursuit of obtaining an income.

What this has done is break up the family nucleus!

When the family is broken either by a dual parent working household, or by the tormenting percentages of divorce and single parenthood, the children are left to fend for themselves – not just in many cases to take care of their basic needs – but as children expected to grow up quick and take on the sole responsibility of making adult decisions.

Who do we blame for this demise, and how do we do what needs to be done and still raise well-rounded and adjusted children? The answer is not a simple one, but there is an answer.

Although time spent as a parent to our children today is pulled from every angle but the home, we must make certain whatever time we have is geared towards the reassurance to our children we are still there for them.

Okay, so how do you make time for the kids as a family or single parent?

I list the following in hopes you can take heed and apply these basic principles to help your child or children adjust to the constraints being put upon you as a parent:

No matter what your day has brought, do not bring it home.

As you leave the office or place of work, leave whatever happened there.

As you begin your commute home, unwind and address any issues that will take you from the arms of your child once you enter your homestead.

If you have calls to return, messages to follow up on, or appointments to make, take care of them if you can before you set foot in the door. If absolutely necessary to do so during the time you should be with your family, set the clock and allow a specified time to do this. Inform your kids that you need to take care of some things. Always let them know that the work that needs attending to in no way is more important than them or affects you desire to be with them. KIDS DO UNDERSTAND IF YOU EXPLAIN THE REASON WHY!

Try your best, perhaps every Sunday evening before your week begins, to set up your calendar for the coming week. Sit with your children if possible during this task and include them so they are aware of what the coming week will be like not only for you, but for them.

As you glance over your calendar be sure to ask your child or children what they have on their agenda. Doing this makes them feel a part of your life even though you may have different things going on that keeps you apart. KIDS HAVE BUSY SCHEDULES TODAY AS WELL!

Don't try to over plan, to compensate out of guilt, the real time you have available for them. The most important thing about being with your kids is being with them. It is amazing how just 1 to 2 hours out of your day dedicated to being with them uncluttered by the television and other whistle and bang activities can create the most important of bonds between your children and you.

As you plan your week, check out the forecast or any other natural event that may be taking place. A picnic under a full moon or a blanket laid out to watch the clouds rolling by on a clear night, can turn into a precious memory that stays with your child forever.

When it rains, it doesn't need to put a damper on your planned outside activity. Bring the time spent together indoors and do things such as art, baking, making homemade pizza (you can get pizza dough from your local pizzeria for under $5.00), doing puzzles or playing games, and bask in the wonder of simplicity and joy with your children.

And last but not least, in these simple points to raising kids as healthy, adjusted adults in today's hustle, bustle world. Always remember no matter how old your kids are, there is no substitute for reading them a story in bed. Snuggle up, read and savor the fact that they will always be your kids no matter how old they are.

"Family can be defined as not having a bloodline, but as those who are a part of your life."

"Children are extremely resilient when it comes to forgiveness, parents should learn from their kids how to forgive."

"A child asks for no more than the time you can give them. Don't overestimate their needs in terms of quantity, give them what you can in terms of quality."

My dear friend, AFFIRM: "Today I take the time to skip stones across a lake with my child. Giving them this time means more to them than a day at the amusement park, because I create the excitement instead of it being created for us."

CHAPTER NINE

DON'T FEAR THE UNKNOWN

"Fear is nothing more than the reluctance to want to grow."

Don't Fear The Unknown

As I stare out at the ocean on this calm night, I am reminded of a journey I embarked upon over twenty-five years ago.

I was living in Victoria, British Columbia, at the time.

The island is a haven for tourist. It is situated at the westernmost point of Canada. This is a commercial fisherman's paradise, offering direct access to its waters where fishing is world renown.

Since its discovery by Captain John Cooke, Vancouver Island has been a prosperous homeland for fishermen and their families.

My best friend was one of those fishermen whose family immigrated to Victoria from Scandinavia.

Lars Erikson's family had come from Denmark, years before my family settled there in nineteen seventy-two, to reap the rewards of these famous waters.

Lars was the youngest of four brothers. We met playing rugby in our senior year of school. Here, our lifelong friendship began.

Although we came from different parts of the world, we shared a common bond with our passion for rugby and the island's beautiful coastline.

When we weren't banging heads in the scrum against our opponents, we would tie our canoe to the top of his truck and set out to explore the island's vast intercostal waterways.

Tough as we were on the field, we looked forward to the serenity of charting the smaller islands northeast of Victoria.

When the summer came around, Lars, as he had done since he was twelve, would accompany his brothers and father, fishing Alaska's waters to learn the skills he needed to one day guide his own commercial fishing fleet.

In nineteen seventy-three Lars Erikson would take on the role of a commercial fisherman and make it his life's vocation.

This was also the year I would begin my own journey to acquire the experiences I would need to help me fulfill my dream of being a journalist and travel writer.

Little did I fathom the summer of our departure from high school would not only be filled with an adventure unlike any I had ever known before, it would become one of the greatest lessons life could ever teach me.

And so, my lesson began.

Dana Erikson was a petite woman in her early fifties. She radiated with a youthful beauty, her natural blonde hair always tied in a flowing ponytail, pulled to one side over the front of her shoulder.

Unlike the stormy, weathered faces of her husband and sons, Dana Erikson had kept herself protected over the years from the elements as she waited her family's safe return from their fishing trips.

Although I was the complete opposite of my blonde haired, blue-eyed friends from Denmark, with brown hair and green eyes, Dana Erikson treated me like one of her own.

Lars and I had accompanied his mom during the school year to bid farewell to the men at the dock. As the ship made its way towards the inlet, we would run out to the tip of Odgen Point and watch the vessels make their way out into the open sea.

School dismissed for the summer. Now, only Dana Erikson and I stood together to watch the last of her sons embark on his new life at sea with the rest of the Erikson men. The trip would last one month.

As I readied myself to enter college in the fall, the days on the calendar began to roll by.

Two days before my eighteenth birthday, I received a call from Mrs. Erikson inviting me over for dinner. She informed me the men were on their way home and it would be nice to have us all together.

Storytelling was a custom when the family gathered to eat. Unlike most traditional families, where men are the storytellers, Dana Erikson was the teller of the stories.
Edgar Erikson was a tall and lanky man with white hair and baby blue eyes. The head of the Erickson family would sit at the far end of the table mesmerized by his wife's tales. She spoke of her childhood in Scandinavia. Although he knew her life firsthand, Mr. Erickson would stare intimately as each word flowed from her lips.

To this day I can still smell the fresh cherry scent rising from the teakwood bowl of Lars fathers' pipe.

The night we celebrated my birthday was different. Mr. Erikson became the storyteller.

"This pipe," he said, "was given to me at the ripe young age of six by my grandfather. It was filled with the same cherry tobacco, smoldering and ready to go."

He chuckled as he reminded himself of that day as a young boy in Denmark.

"My grandfather would pull me onto his lap, grinned from ear to ear and handed me this very pipe."

"Custom has it," Mr. Erikson continued, "In Denmark, when a boy can inhale a flume of smoke from his grandfather's pipe without turning green, he is ready to join his father at sea and learn the trade of commercial fishing."

"It took me six years to get there," he laughed. "That is why I waited until my own boys were twelve before I started bringing them fishing with me."

After finishing his story, Mr. Erikson reached over and handed me a small wooden box with a blue ribbon tied around it. Just then his wife came into the room holding a cake with eighteen, flickering candles.
The whole family burst into a celebrated chorus of "Happy Birthday." I sat there feeling like a million bucks.

After I cut the cake, my buddy nodded his head and told me to open my gift. I untied the ribbon and pulled off the top. As I stared into the black, felt-lined box, a golden needle glistened and wiggled from left to right. I knew exactly what it was. Lars had shown me this magical gift when we first met.

I thought back to the day I noticed the shiny compass sitting on top of the fireplace mantle and asked if I could hold it. As I held it on my hands, Lars told me how his father's best friend had been lost at sea during a fishing trip.

Claude Ryerson's son had given the fine crafted instrument to Edgar Erickson in honor of his father. As I stared at the compass, I turned to Mr. Erikson and asked. "How could you give up such a special treasure, sir?"

"My dad always told me that there was no greater bond than that of two friends who go to battle together. Whether it is on the battlefield of war, the playing field of competition or the sea for survival, that friendship makes us go on in the toughest of times. If one were to lose the battle, the other will rise to the occasion and claim victory in honor of his friend."

Edgar shook my hand and told me he wanted me to have the compass because my friendship with his son reminded him so much of the one he had lost thirty years ago.

He went on to tell me how he felt he was reliving his childhood all over again watching Lars and I grow our friendship. Just them Lars turned to me and presented me with another gift that would change my life forever.

The gift: I would accompany Lars, his dad and brothers on an eleven-day fishing trip that summer.

Although I had never been out in the open sea for that length of time, weathering the elements and fate of the high seas, I knew I was in good hands.

The trip would give me the chance to see what the life of commercial fishing was all about. I would have my own stories to tell my children one day.

Today, when I stand on the shoreline and look at the horizon, I can still see our boat, the hold filled to the brim with fish as we made our way back into the safe hands of Victoria's inlet.

There is something about being on the ocean, when there is no land in sight and nothing but the moon's rays to guide you. You get to see the fear of the unknown in a whole new way.

From my journey I learned that the only reason we fear the unknown is because we never give ourselves the opportunity to discover its mystery.

All fear is lost when we allow ourselves the chance to see and understand just what it is we are afraid of.

Dana Erikson said it best the day she and I stood as the last of her sons left home to take his place with his father and brothers at sea.

I asked. "Mrs. E, do you fear for the safety of your husband and sons when they go out to sea for months at a time?"

She looked at me and explained it this way. "The life of a fisherman belongs to the sea, not the land. If by custom or choice one wanted to be a commercial fisherman, they would have to entrust their life to the very same element they rely on for survival. I put my trust in that sea to keep my family safe. I pray for their return home. My prayers, not fears, have always been answered."

I learned to trust in the sea as well on that trip.

As the twenty-foot waves swept over our boat, all fear I may have had was lost. I understood what Mrs. Erikson was saying that day.

When we allow ourselves to see and understand just what it is we fear, we are able to transform it into a guiding energy.

As the boat rocked back and forth, I learned to look beyond the height of the waves to the heavens. For in those heavens held a power whose light guided.

As the morning sun burst upon the horizon, I felt the sea become my friend forever.

Journey outside of your fear to discover those worlds you have been afraid to explore and live life to its fullest.

My dear friend, AFFIRM: "Today I seek out that which I have feared, and look it straight in the eyes with a sense of calm and courage. In that moment, a power far greater than I will hold me and calm those fears."

"In times of transition, wonderful new beginnings take place."

Our Journey Will Unfold As It Should

Our journey will unfold as it should. Therefore, choose to take in every new experience that comes your way and know there is divine reason and purpose for everything.

In our relationships with others, let it be our desire to practice actions of love and kindness at all times.

When we do not practice these actions and want to know why, we must not look outward for answers but inward. There we are sure to find the source of all discord.

On this journey within we will come to understand what we need to do if we listen quietly and long enough to our thoughts.

In an attempt to find answers, we sometimes paint a picture of what we believe the outcome will look like. That outcome may not turn out the way we imagined.

We will eventually come to know through experience not to see this as failure, but instead something that was given as a gift to learn and grow from.

In times of transition, times when life presents us with change and uncertainty, accept each day as a new beginning.

As we embrace this, we allow ourselves to be more open to learning more about ourselves. Let us know and accept this with an open mind and heart.

We may find old habits and thoughts creeping up on us but that is okay, this is all part of trusting the transitioning process.

Trusting in ourselves to stay strong and focused, but most importantly, letting all worry go and putting our faith into the hands of our Higher Power, we are able to overcome these moments when our wills are being tested.

The strongest foundation we can build to undertake any change in our lives is trust.

Put that into the hands of a power that never fails to take us where we need to be, to live a life of right action and love for ourselves and others.

When we accept change, we are opening our lives to enrichment.

When we welcome new experiences into our lives, we are welcoming the opportunity to build on our strengths.

Make certain to acknowledge each step as a huge success in your willingness to accept, learn and grow.

By sharing our experiences and resources from the lessons we learned, we grow even more.

Our greatest gift is to be able to share what we have learned to help others along their path of renewal and growth. This is how we can live our best life.

My dear friend, AFFIRM: "Today I take all the experiences in my life and apply them as teaching tools to help others along their path in this world. The ones I reach out to help will, in turn, always be thankful for my unselfish guidance."

CHAPTER TEN

BUILDING LOVING RELATIONSHIPS

"When you connect with someone, let it unfold as it is supposed to."

What Is A Soul Mate?

Sometimes we meet someone in life who is a direct reflection of us. This can be a man or a woman. This person can be like us in every way. They see our dreams as we do, think along the same lines about our ideals and approaches to life, possess our qualities and, for the most part, appear as a mirror image of our likes and dislikes.

How wonderful it is to think we have finally met someone who is just like us. In reality this may also scare us and cause us to approach the relationship with apprehension.

Why is this?

I believe Oriah Mountain Dreamer summed this chance encounter up best in her book, The Invitation, in which she writes about mapping our intent to live passionately, and settling for nothing less than what is real.

As I began pondering the failure of my marriage and several relationships afterwards, I felt a common bond between Oriah and me through her words. As I read her poem, I realized that I hadn't known who I was for a long time. The invitations I sent out or accepted for many years were like attending a party where once you walk in the door and look around, you know you don't belong. Yet, I stayed.

In her poem titled the same name as the book, she writes, "It doesn't interest me what you do for a living. I want to know what you ache for and if you dare to dream of meeting your heart's longing."

We all spend our lives hoping to meet that someone who embraces all of our ideals and dreams without question.

We naturally seek a friend or partner who will walk though this world as we do, looking outward in the same direction.

When we meet someone with whom we can sit and feel no resistance to our way of life, we tend to feel good about ourselves and as a natural reaction, want to invite them into our lives for more of this good karma.

Sometimes, because we have been lacking these feelings in our life for some time, we rush headlong into the relationship.

This, in essence, never really gives us a chance to develop the relationship in a way that is healthy for both people.

The term "soul mate" is truly enduring and special. It is one reserved not for a vision we dream and hope of unfolding, but for one that already has.

When we meet that special someone we feel we want to label as "the one rising above all that have come before," understand that there are so many steps to reaching that plateau.

So how do we get to the soul mate stage?

There is the building of any relationship that begins with communication and this starts the friendship.

In the course of that friendship, things unfold about our individual qualities that define not only who we are, but what we want from life.

When we meet someone who attracts us into their life, there is a reason. That reason is not always a divine one, or one of eternal fate. Sometimes someone just comes into our life at a moment when they (or we) need exactly what they (or we) have to offer.

When you know your wants, and understand your needs, it is so much easier to know just why this person has arrived at your doorstep. With this knowledge you will always be true to yourself, as well as them, in your expectations. It all starts with knowing just who you are.

As two people come together in friendship with the desire to form an intimate relationship, knowing your wants and needs allows you to communicate truthfully right from the start.

While we may both want the other to accompany us as we jump into the fires of life without fear, we must first know this is something we are willing to do on our own.

In her poem, Oriah Mountain Dreamer captures the desires of one to be as one with another in all aspects of life, yet for each to bring their individual dreams to the table so that they may be unfolded without reservation and accepted with nothing more than the willingness to share life building those dreams together.

If we are to dance to the same music, we must first hear those sounds in our own heart as the rhythm of life that we dance to.

We can then extend our invitation to another to partake in our heart's song. If this rhythm begins to stir the two hearts together, we have created a harmonious dance as one.

If we are to be on the same page, we cannot be afraid to share the stories that have made us who we are as individuals.

Life lived is infused with pain and disappointment, success and failure, regression and growing.

As we come to the front lines and spill upon the soils the truth about where we have been and who we are, we are able to walk forward leaving footprints of integrity. Honesty and integrity are the building blocks from which strong individuals create strong relationships.

If we are to look outward in the same direction, the course of our lives must be of a path we are both willing to travel, even if neither one of us has travelled that course before. On the course of any relationship there are mountains to climb; each step will be an endearing test of each one's ability to sustain the other.

Courage to do so willingly for one another becomes the lasting strength you build together to face anything in this world.

Belief in one another allows spontaneity. As part of your life it brings renewal to our seasoned souls.

Long-term relationships last because neither one ever listened to anyone who told them it wouldn't!

One of the most beautiful things about two people, is when they come to a point they can look at one another and know the other is their soul mate. To achieve this life has to be lived.

Take the time to get to know one another. As much as you may want to initially make them a part of your daily life, allow the passing of time to tell you if this is really where you want to be and where you belong. Keep with your inner spirit as you move forward and let your heart guide you.

Making someone a part of our daily life is so much more involved than just agreeing to the same things all the time.

It is okay and a healthy part of any relationship to disagree. When this happens, find a place of compromise. Compromise isn't always about having a meeting in the middle; love does call upon us to bear the brunt of the weight sometimes. This is an enduring part of any partnership. We are all called upon to carry the torch, but in the long run we are all winners at the finish line!

I bid you love and happiness in your pursuit of your soul mate. There is that ONE for all of us out there.

We may not see them yet, or they may have come our way at some point in our life when we were unsure of whom we were as a person. This was a good thing, because now you may both have cleared your paths of the obstructions that stood in the way of your being together back then, and are now ready to rekindle that quest to be together forever!

 I have come to know who I am and what I want from life. I have been able to write my own invitation for what I desire in a relationship.

My dear friend, AFFIRM: "Today I define just what my definition of a soul mate is, and I write out my own invitation. I use this to invite that person into my life. If they are already there, I let them know they are the one for me, and share with them how I feel about them."

"Write your invitation to love."

Writing Your Invitation For The Love You Deserve

When we let go of the qualities and traits we desire, the things that we feel are important to our feeling of contentment and overall wellbeing, we are in essence sacrificing the desire to lead a life of happiness and joy.

If you want to be treated a certain way, you deserve to have that. If you love to dance, listen to music, enjoy the arts, but find yourself settling into a relationship with someone who is not willing to share in your enjoyments, you will find yourself lacking in those areas that give you satisfaction.

Two people deciding to be together to share life should be able to bring into the relationship their own qualities and outlets that define them as individuals. If you are expected to leave who you are at the door, you may want to rethink having any long term commitment with that person.

If you and your partner know up front what makes each of you thrive as individuals, whether it be the work you do, hobbies, sports or leisure activities you engage in, tastes in foods or amount of time you set aside for yourself to take care of you, you can build a beautiful partnership. You can grow together as the years pass because you are supportive and respectful of the other's needs.

I am not saying there won't be times you will have to make sacrifices for the other, just as there will be times they may have to set aside their needs for you.

We all have to be willing to compromise for our partners and our families. This is a normal part of being in any relationship.

Compromising is a way of expressing your love for your partner and family. But sometimes compromising just isn't feasible.

As long as we find the way at some point to reciprocate for what others have given up for us, or they reciprocate for what we have given up for them, our sacrifices will always be done willingly and with love.

You have lived the way you wanted, you know exactly who you are, have seen and done what you wanted to appease you in your life as a single person, and now you are ready to set the table for finding that one special person to begin sharing your life with.

Just how can you ascertain if you have come through one or more failed relationships or, at the opposite end of the spectrum, lost a love that gave you the most beautiful years of your life, that you will ever find love again?

You start by taking an inventory of you.

Think of it as having a party and wanting it to be the greatest celebration of life you ever experienced. Would you not want to invite those people that would make your celebration a memorable one?

This is how you create your invitation for love.
Take all the pleasurable experiences you have had in your life and list them with what made them so memorable. Think about the person or people involved. Recall the place or places where you were gathered, and the simple touches that contributed to the wonderful outcome.

I wrote this invitation at a time in my life when I really wanted to see just what I was missing from my relationships.

As I penned my thoughts I began to understand just how we so often short change ourselves in our desire not to find the right love for us, but to be the right love for another.

Go ahead, create your invitation. I created mine.

My Invitation:
This is what I want in my life. Most importantly, balance, and with that a place in my heart and mind that is still and calm every day, even in times when life challenges me.

I want to let go and allow myself to soar to incredible personal heights, and to obtain a world of spiritual and intellectual knowledge I have yearned to digest and grow from for many years.

For that balance, I know there is an important element I have always known, and that is the loving of myself, and the sharing of my loving self with someone else.

What do I want from that someone in my life?

I want us to grow together, yet in our own ways.

I want us to share in a common goal of making each day one that can be reflected upon as one we gave our all to, and received abundance from in all aspects; spiritually, emotionally and intellectually.

I want to feel it as a personal growth as well as a together growth.

I want to give my love in all ways, and feel that love in all ways.

I want to grow and explore on my own and encourage the same in my partner every day.

I want us to make love with a passion that is poetic and spontaneous, slow and gentle, yet wild.

I want to laugh and cry and share all of our emotions comfortably whenever they arise.

I want to be able to argue intelligently where we both present our views without judgment.

I want us to explore the world with wide-eyed wonder and enthusiasm for learning new stuff.

I want that special someone to continue to accept me for who I am, and, that however I need to grow myself, will always be supported, as I will do the same for them.

I want to grow old embracing the idea of an eternal timeframe, yet spend each minute living in the present moment.

I want to hug and kiss in public and hold hands on the couch without saying a word, yet knowing the love is there with just a glance and a smile.

I want balance in my vocation and my day so that I have time enough to work and play and rest without feeling I haven't done enough, and have that special time for my partner.

I want to be able to travel and enjoy a world of new cultures and history.

I want the two of us to travel together and rediscover our love in new and exotic places (even if it is just around the corner, I know we will make it our paradise.)

I want us to pray and embrace our individual, spiritual selves and grow as a couple in God-like ways every day. And when I close my eyes at night, I want to look at my partner and with a soft kiss and hug say. "Goodnight my love, you are a gift to be cherished forever."

My dear friend, AFFIRM: "Today I write my own invitation for whatever I want to invite into my life."

"Find out what others need from you today and provide it with love."

This Is Not A Test, It's LOVE

How often in a loving relationship are we presented with situations that really try us and wear us down?

It would be easy to just throw your hands up in the air and say, "to hell with it!"

This is not a very good way of showing your love.

Love endures all and that endurance is not a test of wills or strength or of the love for one another. Outside circumstances that arise unexpectedly in a relationship that seem to pull us ajar from one another, is something that is part of life and loving someone.

Things pop up in life all the time, things that are out of our hands, and they seem to come when we least expect.

You know the old feeling, merrily rolling along!

Well, life and love are not designed to coast downhill at every giving moment.

Think of love kind of like when you were a kid taking your Radio Flyer down that fresh blanket of snow.

The ride down was fun and exhilarating. The longer the hill, the more you got from the ride. Then after all the thrills you came to a stop at the bottom. You got up off your sled, put the rope in your hand, and proceeded to happily climb back up that hill knowing another breathtaking ride was in store.

This went on for hours without question.

You never stood at the bottom of the hill with your reddened cheeks and snow covered pants, boots and jacket and said, "Heck, I have to climb this thing again?"

Love my friends is very much the same.

Sometimes we are able to park at the top of the hill and enjoy that first ride down without the climb, but if we want to do it again, well, time to trek up that hillside.

Love is not always about the ride down, but about the climb back up.

When life tugs at your relationship, when it throws an unexpected event in your way, this is when real, true love becomes strongest.

Think of the soldier who has to go off to a foreign land leaving his wife and family home, or the business person who has to travel for weeks, or sometimes months at a time, because it is part of their job; the love you have doesn't just get tossed aside, the situation you may have been used to has changed, but the love shouldn't.

So how do you survive when something comes in to your relationship that can cause it to come under strain?

First of all is to accept it! Fighting unforeseen circumstances just makes matters worst.

Sit with your partner and discuss everything happening so you both have a clear understanding of what is needed from both of you.

Bottom line is this: you both have your personality traits, try not to be judgmental of one another's habits, beliefs or approach to life…remember, you accepted them into your life hopefully having taken enough time to get to know these things about one another.

The beauty of the freedom that exists before settling down in any relationship is that we do have the right to make our choices in life.

We can choose where we live, for the most part how we live, our religion or beliefs, our mode of dress, what we eat, to dine in or out, to exercise or not, and for the most part, live a life that is conducive to our liking.

The next time you feel reluctant to be who you are, try this.

Instead of trying to decide how to be, for the sake of others, just be yourself. Not everyone is going to accept you for whom you are, but that is okay. We are all unique in our own ways. This is the beauty of being an individual.

If another person has a hard time accepting you, move on. As the saying goes, "There are plenty of other fish in the sea."

What I learned in my life is this, when we try to please others we shortchange ourselves.

While we may think we are doing justice in catering to the expectations of others, we are merely molding ourselves in the eyes of someone else.

We want to be accepted and liked; this is a natural calling for being human. The key is letting others know, without falsification, our preferences for accepting and acceptance. If I am willing to accept you into my life just as you are, I would want the same from you.

In order to prosper, relationships must be based on openness and honesty. Communication is the key!

This allows us to open the doors in our relationships, which is essential to establishing and maintaining the giving and receiving of thoughts and feelings from you to the other person, and vice versa.

From time to time there may be things going on inside of us that we feel reluctant to share.

Perhaps we are afraid of hurting or chasing someone away from us by being honest with our feelings. This is a natural feeling. When you love and care about another person, the last thing you want to do is hurt or push them away.

For years, I found it difficult to be upfront with others about my feelings. I kept my thoughts locked away, and in the process struggled with my own emotions. I realized the only person I was hurting was me.

In a way, I was being judgmental.

I was judging what the other person might think or feel about what I had to say. Not only was I being unfair to myself, I was being unfair to them. I wasn't giving the other person the right to hear what I had to say and make a decision for him or herself.

If the issue is coming from the other person's side and that person says they need to handle it alone, do not take it personally!

The most ideal situation for any couple would be that they work together to resolve the situation, but this can't always be so.

When one or the other of you needs to go at it alone to face and resolve conflict, the best thing the other can do is show an unselfish amount of love, compassion and understanding for their partner.

Remember, he or she did not ask for this situation to be dumped on their plate.

By allowing the other person to take the time needed to sort out and help fix the problem, you are giving them the best love you can, as well as the utmost respect for their needs.

If that need is for you to back off and leave well enough alone, be respectful and honor that request.

Just because one person in the relationship feels a need to face something alone, it does not mean they are sweeping you out of their life, it just means they have to do what is best for all involved, including themselves.

In this situation, think of yourself as the player on the bench suited up and ready to go when called upon. You may not always get the nod from the coach, but that doesn't mean you can't cheer your team on.

Letting your partner know you are there for them and supportive in any way you can be, may be all they need to hear from you. Words of encouragement like this take the pressure off of your loved one.

Balancing the love for a partner, along with their having to step in and deal with outside problems from family members or others, causes great strains on everyone.

By being the one to offer compassion and understanding instead of a, "what about me" attitude, you are showing your love for them in a very special way. This is called true love, uncompromised and dedicated.

In the end all will work out however it is supposed to, and your relationship will be able to enjoy that wonderful ride downhill.

This time the trek back up will seem effortless and fun. Oh, and it is okay for you to send little reminders that just show you care about and love them.

My dear friend, AFFIRM: "Today I will be upfront with others about my feelings. I won't keep my thoughts locked away for fear of hurting. I will be gentle with my words and use the "I" word rather than passing the blame off on the other person."

"Build your relationship upon patience, trust and communication."

Sustaining Love In Spite Of...

Couples that are able to sustain their relationships year after year in spite of life's pressures have a gift in common.

That gift is, knowing thy self.

The secret to any long-term partnership begins with the self. We must first know who we are as an individual before we can know anyone else.

Make sense? Here, let me put it into perspective.

All relationships begin on a grandiose scale. Smitten with love and head over heels passion, all is like a script from a romantic movie. The true love, the love that survives, is when as they say, "The honeymoon is over."

True love is in knowing thy self and loving yourself and reflecting that outward to another.

True love constitutes respect, trust and most of all, appreciation for your partner.

Life will most certainly change as the relationship grows and both must grow in tune with this.

It is wonderful to see portrayals on the big screen about couples who just can't wait to rush into one another's arms and be swept off their feet, but in reality, a relationship that grows and matures together also endures change.

The love that strengthens is the love that is held together by common threads; respect and a feeling of being in love with your partner no matter what else gets in the way.

What this says about love is that it will survive and endure the tides of change.

Being in love with the one you love means simply, small reminders that he or she means the world to you. As we get caught up in everything going on in our lives, the one constant bond of true love, even when you cannot be there physically to hold that person, look them in the eyes and tell them you love them, is in knowing your love for them and their love for you is strong in spite of everything else keeping you from being together.

A key here is that no matter what may get in love's way, simple reminders and gestures of affection can lift one another's spirits during these trying times. It only takes a second to say, "You are in my thoughts."

Loving relationships are also built upon balance and an understanding of yours and your partner's needs.

We all need time to ourselves, this allows us to rejuvenate.

When we don't take this or give this to our partner, we lose sight of balancing out all that is going on in our lives.

Having obtained this balance, we are now able to face life's challenges. And in rising up to meet those challenges, we build a stronger connection of love and respect for one another.

My dear friend, AFFIRM: "Today I sustain my relationship by finding ways to fall in love as when we first met. If it is worth saving, I do what I have to, to make it last."

"Learn to attract only the best of all things into your life."

Relationships, Chaser, Taker Or Giver

We are given the thought that in order to change anything in our lives from negative to positive, one must find love within and act unselfishly.

Universal law has confirmed, once we recognize love within ourselves, once we begin to feel it radiate from the depths of our emotions, once we accept this feeling as real and begin sharing our souls passion, we open the hearts of others.

Why is it then so many, who have seemed to find love of self, remain unsuccessful in radiating that love outward?

It is not so much that we are unsuccessful at radiating love outward; we fail to see it for what it is, a free-flowing spiritual energy to be treated with care and respect when it comes back to us.

Once love is given as a true conveyance of self, it becomes part of the soul of the universe. Once this energy becomes part of the universe, it flows freely. Flowing freely, this love-energy sets out in search of others in tune with its vibrations.

A person attracted to one giving off this energy feels the attraction simply because they too have set their loving vibrations free into the universe.

Okay, so why is it then what we attract into our realm of life doesn't always succeed?

What we attract has a hard time succeeding because consciously or not, we force our love outward in our efforts to attract those relationships instead of letting the energy of our self-love flow freely on its course attracting the right circumstances to us. In other words, we become the Chaser or Taker or even both!

When we do not allow the natural processes of the universe to take place we are merely trying to gain control of the outcome.

Control is a hard-pressing energy, a negative and disturbing energy that causes emotional circuits to burn out.

The very action of chasing after love causes us to love too hard.

The act of taking that Divine Love from the universe to fill our needs causes us to destroy the love being sent our way.

When our actions take us in either direction, we become blind to the reality that the outcome is the exact opposite of what we perceived our loving energy would bring.

We then slip into a mode of denial because we do not see our efforts at loving as being overbearing, controlling and needy. For some, this control mechanism serves to fill needs others could not fulfill as we were growing up. This is the Taker.

Both the Chaser and Taker create an overbearing and controlling personality. Out of lack of self-love we try to get another's love to become that love of self for us.

Remember, it was the control mechanism that reversed the outcome, not the love that went out. This is what we can come together to see as the laws of attraction.

Have the laws of attraction promised good outcomes from good thoughts for you?

Have you set out thinking good thoughts?

Did you not attract good things?

Then, did you not begin to mettle with the free-flow and all hell broke loose?

When we try to create our own little universe to contain another's love, this act of wanting it all for ourselves will dramatically disturb the outside universe.

Soon shock waves will be piercing our wall of protection, causing it to crumble, and with it, all we tried to capture out of ego and need, will take flight like a captured bird finally set free!

Then we find ourselves alone, love-defeated, and asking how our love could have been given in vain.

Let's go over this concept about love and attraction.

All of us, deep down inside, want to be loved. This is the breath of our existence, the very light that energizes the life within us. Without it, we cannot exist.
We have been raised with a mindset that conditioned us to believe love must be won over.

Through trial and error, we have grown up believing our failures have to be justified.

We seek that justification through chasing after love too hard, or taking from and draining from the love that comes our way, to serve only us.

We try to control the outcomes in our relationships, which disturbs the natural flow of love, which interferes with the law that says if we send out love as a free flowing energy, like will be attracted to us.

But as love comes our way and we try to control it and reel it into our lives for our own purpose, we disrupt this natural occurrence.

Once we tangle with the law of attraction, we create discourse in our life and other lives.

If you want to be successful in attracting and enjoying love so that it sustains and doesn't drain you, love freely and accept love freely into your life without trying to control or define it to fit your meaning and purpose.

Seek balance through a place in your heart and mind that soothes and calms every day. Even when life challenges you, let go and allow yourself to soar to incredible personal heights and obtain a world of spiritual awakening, and yearn to digest and grow from everything you encounter and experience.

Unearth the loving of thyself and sharing of that loving self with all those in your life.

Grow together yet in your own individual ways.

Give praise and thanks for that personal growth as well as the together growth.

Share a common goal of making each day one that can be reflected upon as one you gave your all to, and received abundance from, in all aspects: spiritually, emotionally and intellectually.

Give love to others and feel love from others thankfully.

Grow and explore on your own and encourage the same in others every day.

Love in ways that are poetically expressed and deeply heartfelt.

Love in ways that leave everlasting impressions even when shared for just a moment.

Laugh and cry and share all emotions comfortably whenever they arise.

Argue intelligently where you present your views without judgment.

Explore the world with wide-eyed wonder and enthusiasm for learning new stuff.

Continue to accept one another for who you are, allowing room for growth whenever the need arises.

Grow old embracing the idea of an eternal time frame; yet spend each minute living in the present moment.

Hug with meaning.

Hold hands or just touch fingertips.

Find balance in your vocation and day so that you have time enough to work, play and rest, without feeling you haven't done enough.

Make special time for those you love.

Travel with your children by car and you will discover places together that create a lifetime of beautiful stories and memories.

Take time with your partner to also travel alone so the two of you can rediscover your love.

Give thanks for everything

Live in LIGHT-likeness every day.

When you look into the eyes of those you love, look with your heart into their soul. To get there, just follow the path that leads from their heart, and walk it with yours.

My dear friend, AFFIRM: "Today I stop settling for anything in life that feels wrong in my heart. I do not compromise self-worth and happiness in hopes the situation may change one day. I take action and change the situation for my well-being and happiness."

"Believe God has plans for love in your life, be patient."

Love Is The Word

If it was a road of heavenly bliss taken away without deliberate hurt, such as the passing of your loved one, it may take awhile to feel whole enough again to get on with your life.

When you have been hurt and either been cast away to flourish on your own, or made the decision to put an end to a life of unhappiness, it is so important to tread slowly.

In either scenario, it is only natural to protect yourself and take time to find the right love; if that is what you choose to seek.

Our ancestors believed, for the most part, that we live our life for one mate, and when that mate is gone, we finish out life in his or her memory.

Times have changed.

I've met men and women alike who want, and may have even been asked by their partner, to find someone else and continue loving, even after they have gone on to eternal rest, divorced or even remarried.

This is a beautiful reflection of the love and trust two people shared with the one another.

In the original exchange of vowing to love and cherish one another till that time when God had other plans, the love was strong enough to let go, and ask for a promise the other would not mourn the happiness shared, but instead find a way to love again.

In the case where your relationship was a blessed one, you want to feel a continuance of that love in the eyes of a different soul. There is someone out there for everyone who possesses many, if not more, of the wonderful qualities you were used to having in your life. On the other hand, when an unloving childhood or relationship filled your life, you may have lost all desire to try to love again.

There are some people who go through life pretty much incapable of expressing their love for others.

The reality is this, just because he or she grew up in an environment or suffered through a relationship where there was no hugging or heartfelt expressions of affection for one another, doesn't mean it was not there to be given, they just did not know how to express their loving feelings or felt uncomfortable doing so.

Think of it in these terms as you allow your compassionate side to see it from their point of reasoning; they just never had anyone to give it to them or express it to them.

I believe, and I would like you to embrace this thought as a reflection of my dear friend's conversation with me, Love, is inside of us all to be shared, felt and lived.

When you can tap into and remove the pains that have kept you from loving, you will love and allow yourself to be loved. If you are the loving one, never defray from that outpouring.

In either case, the key is in knowing within that you are a good person, and that no matter what life brings, you will always love yourself. It is okay to be loved and give love again.

In essence, by loving great again you are honoring the person you loved great in the first place. And, by giving love to others in spite of not having love in your own life, you are able to live as a reflection of divine love.

People come into our lives for a reason. They may not stay as long as we want them to, and that is the part most of us have a hard time with.

I recall theses beautiful words by Alfred Lord Tennyson. "'Tis better to have loved and lost than never to have loved at all."

A friend recently sat with me and spoke about, "The Word."

"The Word, what is The Word?" I asked.

"Think about it" she said.

"If there was one thing in this whole world that we would need to survive, what would it be, wouldn't love be our greatest attribute?"

"Wow," I replied. "Love really does say it all doesn't it?"

Let's face it. We all thrive to feel the love of another from the time we first open our eyes. Why should we feel any different at 40, 50, 60, or even 110?

You may not be the one I will be blessed to love for all of our lifetime, as that measure of time is not mine to measure, but you shall always remain in my heart as one I have loved and been blessed with to be loved by, in whatever time we are given.

My dear friend, AFFIRM: "Today I love again. If that love was lost or didn't work out, I know in my heart love is waiting, and I open my arms and heart to receive it."

ABOUT THE AUTHOR

"I write to awaken you to the beauty you hold within you."

The Beginning of How To Be Positive

I published my first book entitled, INSIGHTS, in April of 2011.

On January 22, 2012, I set my sights on turning another dream into a reality.

What started out as a way to connect with the world through my writing soon became the foundation for a goal of creating the book you now hold in your hands.

My writings, I was told, were simple, easy to digest, inspiring, self-help tools.

On February 19, 2012, a vision came to me.

Why not put together the stories and experiences from my life and publish a book. In a way this is an autobiography but in essence, it is a guide to living right.

For those of you who have been a part of my life in one way or another, I am sure while you may have thought you knew me well. Reading this will take you a little deeper into my life and let you know just who I am.

In the process of discovering me I hope you will most importantly, discover yourself.

We have all gone through things in life we wished we could have done differently, after all we are only human. In reflection we see things we know existed all along but were afraid to accept, so we lived in denial.

To bear the soul is one of our hardest choices for anyone to make. There is pain in stripping oneself of the things they have masked, and it is only when we can face our own unveiling that we can lift the burdens that have held us back from our true self.

As I wrote, I grew to know myself better. I learned in this process that only we can short-change ourselves, only we can live the life God intended for us.

On September 5, 2012, at 11:48 pm, the vision for this book became a reality.

I did not do this on my own.

The energy that guided every word came from the light and energy of my Higher Power. It came from others I have conversed with over the years.

I was born to write as a way of aiding others through what I feel within. For now, I let the written word speak what I feel in my heart.

Some of you have expressed wanting to fulfill your own dream of writing a book.

The best advice I can give is this…write about what you are compassionate about, what you love and believe in, what sets your soul soaring, and then, set a goal for yourself and dedicate your energy to accomplishing your dreams with love and passion.